A Travel Guide for Cruises
VACATION

CORNERSTONE LIBRARY · New York

AT SEA

Else and Bennet Daniels

Published by Cornerstone Library, Inc.
A Simon & Schuster subsidiary of
Gulf & Western Corporation
Simon & Schuster Building
1230 Avenue of the Americas
New York, New York 10020

Designed by Irving Perkins
Manufactured in the United States of America
10 9 8 7 6 5 4 3 2 1

"Cornerstone Library" and the cube design are registered
trademarks of Cornerstone Library, Inc., a Simon &
Schuster subsidiary of Gulf & Western Corporation.

Library of Congress Cataloging in Publication Data
Daniels, Else.
    Vacation at sea.

    Includes index.
    1. Ocean travel. I. Daniels, Bennet, joint author. II. Title.
[G550.D36   1979b]   910'.45   79-16917

ISBN 0-346-12423-9

PICTURE SOURCES: Chandris, Inc., 5, 16, 101, 103; Costa Line, 116–117; Cunard
Line, 29, 102; Hellenic Mediterranean Lines Co., Inc., 113; Holland America
Cruises, 9, 20, 37, 42, 79, 95, 106, 111, 126, 140, 153, 155; Home Lines, 16, 24, 89, 90,
120–121; Italian Line Cruises International, 11; Peter Kohler Collection, 107;
March Shipping Corp., 21, 92, 104; Norwegian Caribbean Lines, 46, 125, 129;
P&O Princess Cruises, 8, 28, 50, 97; Royal Caribbean Cruise Line, 78; Royal Vik-
ing Line, iii, 55; Sitmar Cruises, 6, 13, 19, 25, 56, 63, 70, 130, 143, 160; Sun Line
Cruises, 79.

for JW,

who understood the mystique of ships

Contents

Acknowledgments

It is obvious that this book could not have been written without the generous cooperation of many friends and business associates, among them most prominently the members of Cruise Lines International Association. We would be remiss if we did not single out for special thanks a few officials who were especially helpful: David Sutherland at Home Lines, Robin Boyle and David Hoffner at Sitmar, Sandra Schler at Costa, Ann Abitia at P&O Princess, Svetlana Lisanti at Hellenic Mediterranean, Edith Hudson at Norwegian Caribbean, Bob Bebber at Lauro, and Suzanne Haines and her former co-workers at March Shipping. And our favorite crew member, Piero Sorrentino.

Many cruise enthusiasts shared with us their memories, anecdotes, and hints, and we are indebted to them all. But we have most often traded tales of life at sea with Peter Kohler. We'll always be beholden to Jim McCullough and Frances Hawkins, who launched us in the travel business. The aid of the gang at Ober-United Travel has been invaluable; our thanks to Larry Flack, Howard Grant, and, most especially, Max Youmans.

Karen Foster has been an estimable typist: unflappable and accurate.

Madelyn Larsen, our editor at Sovereign, is a true friend; there is no question that this book would not exist without her.

To Luise and Marina, who have had to put up with closed doors and otherwise involved parents while this idea became a manuscript, our assurance that we do appreciate it.

Introduction

The cruise business is booming. More than a million passengers a year now leave U.S. ports for a vacation at sea—a total that a decade ago most travel industry experts would have deemed an impossible goal. The ships in the Caribbean fleet alone contain 25,000 guest beds, about three times the number available in all the hotels in the U.S. Virgin Islands.

The surging popularity of a week or two on a luxury liner is not confined to Americans: In the Mediterranean, in northern Europe, and in the Orient, more cruises are scheduled each season, and the demand for space gallops ahead of its availability. And the entrepreneurs who run the shipping companies are betting big bucks that the trend will continue. Norwegian Caribbean Lines is spending $60 million on the *France* to get it ready for cruises from Miami. Laid up since 1974, the ship—the longest liner afloat—will be rechristened the *Norway* when refurbishing is completed. Carnival Cruise Lines and Home Lines have ordered new ships, expected to be ready for the 1981 Christmas sailings, and Royal Caribbean plans on a new ship that will be ready sometime after that.

Cruise lines are enjoying such prosperity because they have discovered how to take the elements that for more than a century have made a vacation afloat romantic and luxurious and sell them to young working couples and retirees who have never made the Social Register. Cruises today are for everyone, and we hope this book will help open a new holiday world to a lot of fun-seekers who have yet to walk up a gangplank.

In many ways, there's no vacation easier to take than a cruise. Once you have bought your ticket, everything is laid out for you on a silver platter. And we mean everything: sports, entertainment, mountains of delectable food, sightseeing, instruction. And if there's something you want and do not see readily available, there is right at hand someone you can ask to make the arrangements.

But the shipboard world is a different world—that's a good part of its enticement—and getting over some initial unfamiliarity should help you plunge into the fun with all the more abandon. Our goal in the pages that follow is to answer all the questions in the mind of anyone thinking about a cruise adventure, to clear up uncertainties and provide hints for enjoying the voyage to the fullest.

That starts with mating you with just the right cruise—the right length of time, the right destinations, the right ship, and, most important of all, the right ambience. We'll tell you how to check out in advance the tone of a ship, so you won't start off seeking a swinging fortnight of active sports and boogieing till dawn only to find yourself amid the quietest geriatric set on the ocean—or vice versa. There's a packing list, which you can adapt easily to your own wardrobe style. There's a glossary of nautical terms, so you can pass yourself off as an old salt if you want. There are a lot of details about shipboard life, so you won't on the last day of the cruise discover a great little watering spot or pastime that you'll kick yourself for not knowing about sooner. And there's enough about port strategies so you can enjoy the places your ship visits and can shop wisely and well without dropping into Sightseer's Fatigue.

We're drawing not only on our own cruising experience—which dates back to sailings on such lamented beauties as the *Cameronia*, *Queen Mary*, *France*, and *Raffaello*—but also on that of a wide range of other travelers, some world-famous and others well known only to their own family and friends. What we're trying to present is a range of alternatives: There are virtually no "musts" or "must nots," but a lot of hints on how you can find the shipboard life-style that gives you what you, personally, are looking for in your days away from the rat race.

There's a pattern to liner life that spans all the differences in size and nationality that you will find among ships. But it is those very differences that are accelerating the cruising boom. The push is on for ever more variety: more cruises keyed to particular themes, offbeat ports of call—trips to China look like a big growth area—and a greater choice between yachtlike smaller ships and the three-swimming-pool behemoths. The industry as a whole is determined to offer something for everyone.

When we talk about cruise vacations, we mean a trip to sea in a floating pleasure dome. We mean a vacation where you carry your fun with you, and pleasure is an every-hour target. Glossy riverboats are outside our scope. So are freighters that carry a dozen passengers in gentle comfort to exotic foreign ports. We want our ships big enough to have nightclubs and sports decks and the chance to meet someone new and wonderful on your morning constitutional around the deck. At the same time, we'll happily include within our definition of a cruise a transatlantic passage, if the traveler isn't just waiting to get to the other shore, but chooses to go by sea in order to have a vacation en route. (Some ship buffs now will cross on the *Queen Elizabeth II,* spend a day in London, and then come right back to New York on the next crossing.)

Although still thought of by the uninitiated as an expensive vacation choice, a cruise really is a travel bargain. The big advantage is that the price of the ticket covers just about everything—and even the few incidental costs can be figured out ahead, so there are no pocketbook surprises. And the other side of the value equation—what you get for your money—would be hard to match at any landlocked resort, where the additional charges pile up like leaves in autumn.

The truth is, however, that no landlocked resort can give you the extra dimension of your days, and nights, on an ocean liner because the total is more than the sum of the activities and attractions: The very fact that you are *at sea* adds mysteries and marvels that are unique. We try to capture some of that special feeling in this book, but words really won't do it— only by taking a cruise will you see what we mean.

The Perfect Vacation

A World Built for Pleasure

Of all the ways of spending a holiday, a cruise has the most potential for turning into a magical experience. A vacation at sea—one week or longer gliding from port to port on a luxury liner—may not be quite all things to all people, but as a way of breaking the year's routine of work and domesticity, it comes closer than any other.

"Someone has written that traveling by sea most nearly approximates the bliss of babyhood," Geoffrey Bocca, expert chronicler of the good life, once noted. "They feed you, rock you gently to sleep and when you wake up, they take care of you and feed you again.

"Put another way, to step off the West Side of Manhattan onto an ocean liner is the nearest sensation in the world to dying and going to heaven. One has moved into a different form of awareness, with different hallucinatory sights, sounds, smells. Especially smells: Havana cigars, Paris perfumes, and new metal fixtures mixed with the slightest dash of diesel oil and cotton waste."

Genevieve Antoine Dariaux, another expert on the life of the pampered class after her years as *directrice* of the French fashion house of Nina Ricci, puts it more succinctly: Ship travel, she says, "is one of the last orgies of luxury that has survived in our age of interplanetary rockets."

But the beauty of a cruise is that it is, as the title of the Joe Cocker album says, Luxury You Can Afford. While cruising was once the province of only the monied—and, more precisely, the monied with ample time at their disposal—today it is a treat within reach of any working stiff willing to salt away a few bucks every week for a grand vacation. And while the aura of elegance still pervades life at sea, cruising as the seventies become the eighties has loosened up enough so that off-the-rack

3

multi-use clothes will serve you very well, and the steak-and-potato eaters will find plenty on the menu to please their palates.

Cruising today is elegance in a casual mood. "Ocean air and the rhythmic roll of waves are still relaxing, but cruising has come down to earth a little," Rosalind Massow, a contributing editor to l'Officiel magazine, has found. "The glamour is still there, only now the fun is available to a wider spectrum of travelers, from lower-middle-class folk to oil-rich nabobs." Despite the change, she says, "taking a cruise is still like going to a wedding party every day. Passengers are indulged with food, rich desserts, and nonstop activities—from morning calisthenics to late, fun-filled nights."

With a host of lines in the business and a wide variety of ships, itineraries, and on-board styles, any vacationer can find a cruise to match his or her desires. There are voyages to exotic distant lands and those that never get away from ports where the Stars and Stripes flies; those that take sight-seeing superseriously with visiting scholars aboard to brief passengers, and those that emphasize nightlife, shopping, and sandy beaches; trips on which, as one observer puts it, "the blue-hair-rinse concession does its best business," and those that cater to swinging singles. If you are looking for elegance with a capital E, that can still be found.

The one common denominator is that a cruise is dedicated to fun. Whatever your definition of fun is, you can probably find a cruise built around the idea. And because a cruise takes place in a very special, partially isolated world—moving along its own path and unconnected to the land masses that define our daily existences—pleasure can be the dominant motivating force. This isn't a hotel that tries to get you breakfast in bed while it hassles with a policeman over the illegally parked delivery truck out back; this isn't a mountain resort where the newsstand is supplied each morning with the latest evidence of foreign wars and gyrating stock prices. This isn't, in short, a place where the turbulence of the workaday world is constantly threatening to intrude on your vacation. This is a universe virtually unto itself, dedicated to pleasing you.

Which, of course, doesn't mean that it is totally cut off from news of the outside world. Ship-to-shore telephone service and radiograms can put you in touch with colleagues back on land should the need arise. And ships pick up—and usually relay to all passengers—daily news reports broadcast by government radio stations. But at sea, all this information

can take on the nature of data from a distant planet: You hear it, but it isn't quite relevant to your existence right now.

The emphasis on a cruise on creature comfort definitely does not mean that all you can do is loll in the sun and be pampered with midmorning bouillon and frothy rum drinks as the sun slips below the yardarm. A ship lets you be as vigorous as you want to be, athletically or socially. There is a constant round of shows, movies, lectures, and classes available; swimming, exercise rooms, games, and contests are there, as well as two or three pulsating night spots. There are sumptuous meals. And there are the manifold diversions of the ports of call.

It is the get-away-from-winter tropical voyages—particularly those from Florida to the various Caribbean islands and South American cities—that come to mind first when the word *cruise* is mentioned. And with more departures from more U.S. cities as well as San Juan and Nassau, and new harbors being added to the itineraries every year, they offer endless enticing alternatives to snow.

But there are summertime cruises as well, up the North Atlantic coast of the United States and Canada, or through the majestic scenery of Norway's fjords. All around the Mediterranean, from Málaga to Haifa, are marvelous sights that can be visited on a cruise. The fascinating Greek islands are accessible only by ship.

You can take a tour of Europe by cruise, picking an itinerary, for instance, that sails from England to Antwerp, Copenhagen, and Oslo. You can buy a tour package that includes a cruise along with land travel; one example: Fly to London, from there sail down along the coast of France and Portugal and into the Mediterranean, stopping at Barcelona, Cannes, and Genoa, then going overland to Florence and Rome before flying back

to the United States. Want something farther from the beaten track? You can cruise from Hong Kong to Mombasa. Visit the Galapagos Islands. Cruise from Miami to Manta, Ecuador. If water touches the spot, there's probably a cruise that calls there.

But what a cruise is *not* is simply a way to get to those ports. Anyone looking at a cruise as simply a way to get to someplace is missing the point entirely. The ship *is* the someplace. It's your carrier, but also your destination. "The most sensible way to think of an ocean liner is not as a means of transportation, but as a hotel," Mary Scott Welch says in one travel guide. "Picture one of the top-flight money-is-to-be-spent type resorts, where your biggest problem is which pool to lounge around between eleven o'clock bouillon and one o'clock lunch."

The very essence of a cruise vacation—the aspect that makes it unique—is that you stay put while the scenery changes. It is a distinctive combination of many vacation joys, often put together with a particular kind of vacationer in mind. We talk more in later chapters about the variety of special-interest cruises, but their scope is virtually limitless. There are voyages built around hobbies—bridge, cooking, photography, motion pictures, ballroom dancing—and those particularly heavy on entertainment. Country and western music is featured on some trips; such classical music artists as Lili Kraus, Philippe Entremont, James Galway, and the Vienna Chamber Orchestra on others; full stagings of such shows as *Hello, Dolly!* and *The Odd Couple* on still others. There are cruises based on religious faith—an annual sailing from Ireland to the Augustinian missions in Africa, for instance, or a group of eminent rabbis and Jewish scholars gathered aboard ship by the Union of American Hebrew Congregations. And there are those based on human failings: a dieting cruise, a stop-smoking cruise, even a "cruise without booze" sponsored by Alcoholics Anonymous.

"A cruise is many things wrapped up in one nice package," explains Joseph Watters, vice-president of Princess Cruises, a U.S. operation of the giant British Peninsular & Oriental Steamship Co. "The transportation, the cuisine, the new experience, the change of pace, the destination, the entertainment, and much more. People that cruise like the fact that there are no surprises. Virtually all the expense is covered up front and it's a relaxing vacation with no packing and unpacking."

That view is seconded by another steamship company executive, Ric

Widmer, marketing director for Norwegian Caribbean Line (NCL). "Passengers may participate in lots of activities or rest and relax; there's privacy and intimacy plus a chance to be sociable," he says. "The atmosphere is formal or informal and there's the opportunity to let themselves go or to maintain control. The social environment aboard a ship is thought to be unique. It's a safe environment for making new friends, a romantic setting, and good value for the money."

To back up that last point, Widmer trots out a telling statistic: When the line asked passengers after a trip what they thought about the price they paid for what they got, a whopping 75 percent replied that they felt they had received a lot for their vacation dollars. And Hal Gieseking, managing editor of *The Travel Advisor*, says that "the cruise line industry ranks among the most honest segments of the entire travel industry." When he checked with government consumer protection agencies, he found they were "deluged with irate letters about hotels and tours," but that "relatively few complaints have been received about cruise lines."

A major reason for the satisfaction of cruise passengers is that the ticket is really an all-inclusive price. It includes all essentials and most of the happy fillips besides. Your room, of course, and the transportation from port to port. All meals. And that means *all* meals: breakfast, lunch, dinner; midmorning snack, midafternoon snack, midnight buffet; plus fruit baskets delivered to your cabin or any other special gastronomic needs you might have between the six scheduled repasts. And it means anything on the menu at all these meals, and as much as you want. Plus most anything that is not on the menu and that you think to ask the chef ahead of time to prepare. There's no extra charge for any of it. (An exception: As the price of the best Russian black caviar has skyrocketed, one line we know of has started charging extra for that. But it's a rare exception.)

The single ticket price also includes all the entertainment, which means at least one floor show a night—often two—plus at least one new movie a day, plus dance lessons and bridge tournaments and golf instruction and concerts of classical or pop music. Plus dancing-till-dawn night spots. Plus the personal attention of a huge crew charged with nothing but keeping you happy.

The minimal extras are what you would expect. Your purchases in the ship's stores (souvenirs and such forgot-to-packs as razor blades or sun-

tan lotion) or in ports of call, whatever you spend gambling at bingo in an on-board casino, guided short trips (although there's no extra charge for these on a few ships), and most of your alcoholic beverages (there will be at least one free cocktail party, and complimentary wine at gala dinners and at all meals on some French ships). On most lines, your waiters and room stewards will expect tips. And that's it. The unknowns that can break your budget on land trips—when the modest little restaurant you picked for dinner turns out to be the town's most expensive—are completely absent on a cruise.

More than one million Americans a year now think that adds up to a good deal. And even though there aren't accurate figures on just how many vacationers are leaving from foreign ports every year, it is clear that cruising is booming worldwide. Even a conservative estimate would put departures 50 percent ahead of as recent a year as 1974.

Although mass popularity is a new phenomenon, cruising is not. William North, a self-confessed cruising history buff, dates the first such voyage as 1884, a Mediterranean journey on the *Lady Mary Wood* just four years after regular transatlantic steamship service had been established. William Makepeace Thackeray wrote about that cruise in *Notes of a Journey from Cornhill to Grand Cairo*. The itinerary on the early cruises was not set in advance, but varied at the whim of winds, currents, and captain, and the entertainment consisted of the books in the on-board library. But the basic idea was there: a sea journey taken not to reach a distant land, but for its own sake.

Until 1921, although an occasional ship such as the *Arandora Star* was devoted exclusively to cruising, cruises were generally offered only as an off-season variation on a ship that spent most of the year in transoceanic trade. But after the new U.S. immigration law "drastically reduced the immigrant trade," North says, "many ships were sent cruising. Around-the-world cruises, in particular, became popular." Another legislative triumph of the 1920s—Prohibition—also stimulated the popularity of vacations at sea, and some lines began to specialize in what were popularly called "booze cruises" to nearby, and wet, Havana. An estimated fifty thousand passengers took cruises in 1928, and, despite the Depression, that number had doubled by 1937. After World War II, cruising, although still the province of the well-to-do, reached out to many more vacationers. North counts twenty-six ships built expressly for cruising between 1964 and 1974.

Nonetheless, there's still an army of vacationers out there that not only has never gone on a cruise, but that actively spurns them. There are obviously good reasons for going on other kinds of vacations—to see relatives, or inland sights and cities, or to explore one particular place in more depth than the few hours of a cruise stop will allow—but much of the hesitation some folks feel about cruises is based on misinformation. NCL's Ric Widmer lists five apprehensions held by noncruisers: fear of (a) boredom, (b) costliness, (c) a need to be dressy and formal, (d) forced participation in a variety of activities, and (e) seasickness. We have a lot more to say about all of these in the chapters that follow, but the basic answer is that it just isn't so. It certainly isn't so if you level with your travel agent about just what appeals to you and what kind of vacation you want, and the two of you work together to pick a cruise that fits that prescription.

Except for a few safety precautions, no one on a ship is going to muscle you into doing anything you don't want to do. The central spirit of a cruise is that it's pleasure time, when every passenger can follow his or her own piper. But judicious choice of ship and itinerary can ensure that what you want on this particular vacation is also what the majority of your fellow passengers want; even if it is being alone and undisturbed.

Even the risk—slight with today's medications—of being seasick can be minimized with the right choice of ship (big), cabin (central and low), season (avoid hurricane time), and route (stay in calm seas, avoiding travel on the open ocean).

And boredom? It's tempting to rewrite Dr. Samuel Johnson's aphorism, "When a man is tired of London, he is tired of life," to apply to shipboard life. We think that just watching the endless variations in color as the ship cuts through the blue of the ocean is fascinating, but if it is the pleasures of a landlocked resort that turn you on, there are sports, classes, and nightclubs there for the going. The romance to be found in that much-touted novel you've always wanted to read or in the charms of a newly made acquaintance are all there, heightened. In her guidebook *Travel for Lovers*, Carole Chester says, "I can think of no more perfect setting than a windswept deck under a bruised purple sky, where the stars tearfully gleam and the shadowy outline of volcanic islands may or may not be misty hallucinations."

All it takes to make a cruising fan out of a doubter is a few hours of that enchantment. William Lally, maritime reporter for the Baltimore *News-American,* tells how his wife had such misgivings about a recent cruise—her first—that she was ready to turn around and leave until the moment that the *Odessa* actually pulled out of the slip. "But about twelve hours later, my wife's apprehension was dispelled completely," Lally says. "When we awoke the next morning following a pleasant evening in the dining room and show lounge, our eyes were drawn to our stateroom's window and the royal blue waters of the Gulf of Mexico.

"The blue water mixed with the white wash of the ship's wake to turn the water a beautiful shade of turquoise. The sight entranced us throughout the voyage. From that point on we were convinced we had never found a better way to relax."

Ultimately, being at sea is special, a condition different from our daily lives. A vacation on land can be memorable; one at sea is sure to be. Georgia Hesse, as travel editor of the *San Francisco Chronicle*, has done more traveling than most of us can even dream of, yet she says, "I remember every ship trip I've taken with affection and nostalgia. A ship is the embodied spirit of adventure. As the ties to the land loosen, the familiar world—while it shrinks to the size of the ship—simultaneously expands to the ends of the earth.

"I have never sat in a ship's salon, wishing someone else bon voyage, without wishing that I, too, were going."

2   The Lure of a Cruise: It Lets You Be You

There are a host of reasons why vacationers decide to go on a cruise. But the main one is probably that, in the words of Stephen Birnbaum, "it feels bloody marvelous."

Birnbaum, travel editor for the "Today" TV show and a sort of one-man travel conglomerate with a new line of guidebooks, a column in *Esquire,* and regular appearances on both NBC and CBS, insists that "there's a certain peace that comes from having an entire ocean between you and the world's intrusions, and the experience of standing on the stern of a sleek ship as the sunset turns the sky into a red-hued kaleidoscope is like no other. It's enough to make you feel like the only person left in the world—at least until it's time to go in to dinner."

The physical isolation of a ship at sea is perhaps the single most important quality making a vacation at a floating resort different from one at a land-bound get-away haven. The rest of the world is available if you want it, but it doesn't intrude. When fans of cruising talk about why they like shipboard holidays, it is this special opportunity to unwind, to luxuriate, that they usually mention first. And, again, it is this special sense of isolation that makes even the shortest cruise a more complete getaway than an equivalent vacation on land.

Ric Widmer at Norwegian Caribbean says, "People who cruise tell us that vacations at sea offer a blend of pleasures. It gets them away from obligations, it takes the work out of vacations, they are nurtured and treated well, and it gives them a lot of choices."

The need for an extended stretch of real relaxation is important to us all in today's hectic family and work environments. "If the pace of time is becoming so unavoidably furious, then it should be increasingly vital to structure that time in the most beneficial manner possible," two doctors, Stephen A. Shapiro and Alan J. Tuckerman, explain in a recent study of the psychology of vacations. They insist that "the vacation period must be made as valuable and as fulfilling as it can to help achieve a greater tolerance of the accelerated pace of modern life," and that "vacationing in this taut world is not a luxury; it is a necessity."

Shapiro and Tuckerman argue that "doing nothing is an integral part of self-renewal." They consider the desire for a relaxing holiday "a very real need within everyone. It enables a person to hear the voice of the inner self with a special clarity. Most of one's life is spent responding to the needs of others, to the imposed schedule of the workday, the school day, the demands of children or the commands of community membership. But after these calls are answered, there is little time left to just relax."

That's why many people pick a holiday at sea. "It's more relaxing than any other vacation I've ever taken," says Susan Smith, who works for a power company in Atlanta. "On most trips you need a week to recover when you get back." Mickey Nunes, who runs his own business in Woodbridge, Connecticut, explains that the pampering he gets on a cruise is just what he needs to ease the tensions of entrepreneurial life; he and his wife, Betty, have taken well over a dozen cruises. They say they have lost count of the precise number.

"What was I expecting from the cruise?" Margaret Ross of Simi Valley, California, asked rhetorically after a recent journey on the *Danae*. "Good companionship, good guided tours in countries, and relaxing shipboard activities. I found all three." Mrs. Eddie Albert, the wife of the actor, says that she finds shipboard life so close to "paradise" that its glow lasts long after her reentry into the hurly-burly of the real world.

Robert W. Stock, onetime travel editor of the *New York Times*, points out that "for singles of all ages, and both sexes, a cruise ship has special appeal. It is a universe unto itself, a time and place torn out of the context of everyday life—an opportunity to cut loose from cares and conventions. For many, an abundance of sun, food, alcohol, and like-minded companions does the trick."

"In many ways, shipboard life is unreal," says paperback writer Carole Chester. "You may never see the people you meet again, so that confidences are given more quickly than usual and acquaintances are made fast."

We know of one woman in her mid-thirties, happily unattached at the time, who pulled out of a secret corner the wedding ring from a long defunct marriage and included it as part of her cruise wardrobe. She figured that men would be more likely to flock around a married woman traveling alone than a single woman, who might be looking for a relationship that would last past disembarkation. The ploy worked for her, but we've certainly seen plenty of clearly single women—and a few who shucked their wedding rings—who find that condition no liability in shipboard socializing.

Today, when sexual strictures have all but disappeared, the old image of a shipboard romance developing as it never could on land probably does not quite reflect reality. But the special lure of the starry night, of the breeze that encourages two human beings to move closer together, of the days without cares or obligations still holds. If morals today let affairs develop on land, the atmosphere still gives events a little special help at sea. The heightened romance can be with your traveling companion, or with someone you met on deck only that day. And it is a relationship in which you can be whatever you want to be.

There is wine and laughter and music stretching just as long into the night as you want to dance. And the cabins are right there: no driving and no hassles. Jonathan Fox, who served for a time on the staff of a ship that attracted a lot of singles, says that one common signal worked out by roommates was a rubber band around the door handle; it meant that the room was occupied, and that intrusions were most unwelcome.

But a cruise also offers special opportunities to those not traveling alone. We all know the tensions that can develop when several people who actually like each other very much try to decide how all of them will spend a day—especially a vacation day, which is supposed to be time devoted shamelessly to self. Even in a loving twosome, the mountains-or-seashore debate is so common as to become a cliché, and that problem is

just multiplied when you try to make a vacation out of, say, a big family reunion. There are always those who want every hour planned and those who don't want to think beyond right now, those who want a constant round of strenuous physical activities and those who want to move as few muscles as possible, those who want to read uninterrupted hour after uninterrupted hour and those who want vigorous play.

The joy of shipboard life is that everyone can go at his or her own pace, pursuing his or her own pleasure, and yet you are all, always, at the same place: the ship itself. You share the cabin, you share the table at mealtimes, and you can each freely gallivant in different directions the rest of the time without anyone feeling deserted or left behind. It is a particularly ideal arrangement for bridging the generation gap—for parents and children, or for grandparents who want some special time alone with their children's children—because the young ones can go all over the ship on their own, in complete safety. Neither they nor you are fettered.

The great variety of alternatives available on a cruise ship can satisfy not only different persons, but the same person on different days, in different moods. The tiredest of big-city workers, sure that all they want on a vacation is to lie in the sun and do nothing, may start to itch for some more activity after a few days, and on a ship the deck tennis courts and the discos are always there. You don't have to program your schedule to what is being offered, because there's an endless round of possibilities.

But even though we preach that a cruise can be whatever you want it to be—that there's no firm mold you have to try to fit yourself into—let us also urge you to partake of the pleasures spread out there before you. Don't spurn the disco just because you don't do *that* kind of dancing back home; don't stay away from the games deck just because you were always the last one picked for the team when you were a kid.

An incident on a Caribbean cruise in 1975 points up beautifully what we're trying to say. The voyage was sponsored by the New School for Social Research, and more than 350 adult students took lessons from such notables as Eugene McCarthy, David Schoenbrun, Allegra Kent, and Viveca Lindfors as their ship plied from island to island. But one of the most popular courses was given by a lesser-known professor, Dr. Penelope Russianoff, a New School regular. It was called "Risking Change." Trying to explain its attraction for the passengers, one woman said to a *New York Times* reporter, "After all, isn't that what cruises are all about?"

It doesn't have to be, but it surely can be. In the hermetically sealed world of shipboard life, you can be anything you want to be, and if your life until now suggests that it's time for a change, there's no better place to try out a new you than on a cruise. On a cruise, you can pick a personality and roll with it; even if you decide not to keep living that new life when you get back to home port, it's been a very special week or two truly away from the cares, or even the caresses, that shape your land-locked life.

We mean this most sincerely. It's supereasy to meet people on a liner, and you can meet them on whatever terms you want. There are persons who have always hated the fact that they come from a small town in the Midwest. So introduce yourself as being from Chicago or St. Louis or, if you think you can carry it off, Paris or Rio de Janeiro. There's nothing wrong in a traveling salesman who thinks his job is dreadfully dull suggesting that he runs the operation instead; he might do better at it than the guy who now serves as company president. If mousy brown hair always seemed a liability, bring along a shampoo-in red tint and start the trip with a new coiffure.

Approaches can be changed as well as hair color and biographical details. The kind of people who have always envied the lack of inhibition in those who don lampshades at parties can gear themselves up to be just that sort for these few magic days. And, similarly, those who always felt bad the next morning about the way they cavorted the night before can take elegance and refinement as their keywords for the length of the cruise.

We're not preaching that dissembling is a virtue, but merely pointing out that a real you may get buried in the minutiae of day-to-day life. A cruise is an excellent time to risk the change of bringing that persona to the fore. The veracity of little details of your other life that you exchange with new friends—how exciting your job is, how monied your family, how prestigious your schooling—is just not important.

Such little deceptions can cloak in newfound prestige travelers who feel they have not yet achieved the station in life that they really want. But, as Drs. Shapiro and Tuckerman point out in their study of the psychology of vacations, a new identity can be just as appealing to "those who have the 'highest' social standing." Persons who are always tied to their professions, who are forced in every social situation to act the role

of "the doctor" or "the judge," Shapiro and Tuckerman maintain, find a real relief in not having to diagnose the ills of a new acquaintance or listen to a harangue about how street criminals get sentences that are too light. Passing oneself off as an insurance-company actuary can be a step toward relaxation.

It's a good time to play the extrovert. Chester suggests that, even if no friends have come to see you off, you "wave to everyone on the dock anyhow." Frances Koltun, the author of *Complete Book for the Intelligent*

Woman Traveler, insists that aboard ship it is perfectly proper etiquette to barge right in. "Don't worry about the proprieties," she counsels. "Put aside your childhood admonition not to talk to strangers. In these circumstances, it is perfectly correct to take the initiative."

Etiquette expert Amy Vanderbilt has pointed out that this follows the old rule that "the roof is the introduction." Just as diverse guests at an English country house for a weekend could consider themselves formally introduced to each other because they were all under the same roof, so can passengers who are, literally, all in the same boat. "Congenial people usually introduce themselves to one another in short order aboard ship," she wrote.

If you have any amateur entertainment talents, bring along your banjo, marked cards, or sheet music and sign on for the show in which the passengers entertain each other. Throw into your suitcase a costume that will knock them dead at the masquerade party—and make everybody feel they know you in the days afterward. It's a time to unlace a few inhibitions.

If your ordinary life is more sedentary than you like, take the *sportif* tack aboard ship. Enter the sports tournaments, turn out for lessons from the traveling pros who are part of the crew of so many of the larger liners, visit the gymnasium. When you climb into your jogging suit and take off around the deck—every ship will let you know how many laps to a mile—you'll run into other like-minded exercisers.

But if the bottom line on the attraction of taking a cruise is that you can make it into any kind of vacation you want it to be, it follows that you don't have to slip into an outgoing personality if you don't want to.

Cruises are also an excellent time to find some alone time. Take along the copy of *War and Peace* you have been intending for ten years to lace into, or five new selections from the Mystery Guild. If your life on land is one of ringing telephones and interrupting children, the greatest luxury may be to move from clue to clue to solution in one continuous read. Or to stand in your own private corner on an aft deck, watching the wake from the ship meld imperceptibly into the endless ocean waves, and think deep thoughts—or none at all.

You have, the vacation doctors insist, "an obligation to renew yourself and, thus, become a better social companion. Solitude is not, in any sense, a luxury; it is a periodic necessity."

We're not for a moment suggesting that cruises are only for those who are dissatisfied with the person they see in the medicine-cabinet mirror every morning back home. Probably more travelers want their travels to be an extension of their personality rather than a switch, and on shipboard the options are there for them in abundance. One of the best opportunities a cruise offers is to get to know again, really well, one special person from whom the Fates have conspired to keep you too far too long—even if you both have been living under the same roof.

The point is that you will get a lot more out of your vacation at sea if you decide just who you want to be and what you are looking for in those floating days under the sun. Chances are you will be traveling with someone else, perhaps with a group of friends. Decide before you board whether it is an all-for-one-and-one-for-all kind of vacation in which you stick together for all activities, or whether each of you is going to go a separate way. The former can provide the fun of shared experiences, the latter a greater opportunity for individuality. Either can be a prescription for a successful vacation, but not deciding on the ground rules can lead to resentment or boredom when, aboard ship, everything should be nothing but pleasure.

You can live a rigorous life: up at dawn, off to exercise class, count the laps in the pool, hold yourself to one glass of wine at dinner. You can live a go-go-go life: see new sights, learn new skills, make new friends. You can live a wine-wooing-and-song, dance-the-whole-night-through, never-laughed-so-much kind of life. Or you can get to know your inner self better. The potpourri of possibilities is staggering. To pick and choose, all you need is to know who you are. Or, rather, who you want to be.

3 Look Who's on the Passenger List

The heart of what a cruise is—the lolling luxury as you travel from one interesting sight-seeing spot to another—hasn't changed in the roughly hundred years that the pastime has been a popular one. But the passenger lists have.

Twenty years ago, some of the trips taken by such Cunard liners as the *Caronia* were nicknamed by the staff "mink and diamond cruises" so peopled were they with nobility and millionaires. "Practically every night some passenger would book the ship's beautiful Verandah Restaurant and have it decorated according to the geographical mood—South American, Indian Ocean, or Hawaiian," recalls Donald MacLean, captain of the *Caronia* at the time. The hosts would invite two or three dozen of their peers in for a predinner cocktail dance and "guests were expected to turn up in the 'rig of the evening.' "

Today, passengers are as likely to use a shawl they knit themselves as a mink to keep the nighttime breezes off bare shoulders and, more to the point, shipboard friendships are based on how well you like a person, not whether your parents knew each other. "Because America's life-styles have changed and leisure time and entertainment are much more informal, shipboard life on our cruise ships has followed suit," explains Piergiorgio Costa, director of the cruise line that bears his family name. "Dress is more casual, the general atmosphere less formal so that people of all backgrounds and means are very comfortable on board."

That mix of backgrounds—that bringing together of persons of different ages, different occupations, from different parts of the globe—is one of the things that make a vacation at sea special. When Beth Bateman, a reporter for *Travel Weekly,* took a voyage on the *Aquarius* from Athens recently, she found that "the cruise attracted a wide assortment of travelers, including American, French, German, Japanese and others—all of whom seemed to have different reasons for taking the trip. Some came to see the ruins from ancient and medieval civilizations, some to see a different culture, while others came aboard just to relax."

Even cruises leaving from U.S. ports will attract a variety of nationalities. Florida departures usually include a number of South Americans, especially in the summer, when they travel to the United States to avoid their cold months, and often include a cruise in their vacation doings. Paquet Cruises has a special program to attract Europeans to its Caribbean voyages on the *Dolphin*.

And with the growing popularity of special combination fares that tie together the cruise and the airplane trip to the port, cruises are no longer drawing primarily from the states surrounding the trip's point of origin. The trend "has significantly shifted the geographics of our cruise passengers," says Norwegian America's Patrick Kirkpatrick. "Californians, for instance, are very big on flying to Europe to join a cruise." They are also very big on flying to eastern U.S. points to board a ship. Of those taking

advantage of the package fares to Fort Lauderdale to board Sitmar Cruises' Caribbean voyages, 25 percent come from the Golden State.

One of the biggest changes the 1970s informality has brought to cruising is the burgeoning numbers of younger cruise passengers. Cruises have long been popular with honeymooners—with Sunday departures from New York, the *Volendam* has recently been counting as many as 100 honeymooners among its 700 passengers. But now they are attracting in increasing numbers singles in their twenties, career couples, and families with young children.

"The age group is getting younger as these people learn of cruise amenities," Harold Bregman of Harvey Travel, Inc., says he has found of clients at his Houston agency. "Many ships have a series of sports events, and the evening entertainment often features four or five happenings. Some ships have counselors to watch over young children as more families take cruises."

All lines welcome such passengers, but some aggressively aim their marketing patterns at seeking them out. Robert Dickinson, a vice-president of Carnival Cruise Lines, claims that his ships attract passengers who are, on the average, ten to fifteen years younger than those on some of the more formal ships. They are pulled in by the noontime picnics on deck, the extensive casinos (including roulette wheels, which many other shipboard casinos do not offer), the emphasis on postmidnight boogieing, and booking plans that match passengers traveling alone with others (of the same sex) so they can save money by sharing two- and four-bed cabins instead of paying for a single.

The old cliché that the preponderance of passengers on a cruise will be members of the Social Security set is true only of longer voyages, lasting twenty days or more. "Certainly, older and more wealthy consumers take the more expensive cruises, while younger and less wealthy people take our short cruises," acknowledges Costa. "However, there are so many exceptions that the general rules no longer apply. For example, on our most recent around-the-world seventy-four-day cruise, we had a number of twenty-year-old secretaries."

It is not just the length of the cruise that determines the passenger mix: Ships have very definite personalities that attract certain kinds of passengers. Some schedule a disproportionate amount of their entertainment for the late-night hours; that's a good sign that a younger crowd is going to be on board. Others purposely lean toward a bit more formality, acknowledging that their sales efforts are more successful with an older crowd, looking for less bustle. The ship lines carefully "position" each cruise in a specific demographic market, and although there are always, as Costa says, exceptions on the passenger list, most of the voyagers are going to be of the age and personality the trip was designed to attract.

For all the reasons we have already detailed—the security of all-inclusive pricing; the pick-your-own-pace ambience; the new diversity of routes and ports; the sheer *fun* of it all—cruise lines are managing to tap important new markets. Royal Caribbean finds that a whopping 71.5 percent of the passengers on its one-week voyages are taking their first cruise; even on its two-week cruises, which tend to attract those who have tested the vacation idea and find they like it, 51.3 percent of the travelers had signed on for their first vacation at sea.

Even staider, more expensive lines—the kind that traditionally depend on repeat business—are finding a surge in new business from travelers who have never tried a cruise before. Royal Viking Line, for instance, reports that close to one out of five of its passengers is now a first-timer.

Other studies knock holes in other stereotypes about cruise passengers.The bustling variety of activities is a lot more apt to attract retirees than vacationers in their more active years. A new psychological research study underwritten by Norwegian America found that "rest, relaxation and a chance to get away from the routine ranked highest among cruise motivations for Caribbean passengers, and especially among younger people who seek escape from day-to-day tension," according to Pat Kirkpatrick, the company's manager for North America. Folks wanting a cruise "also highly rate the chance to be pampered and treated like a king or queen as a strong motivation for selecting a cruise vacation," Kirkpatrick adds.

The diversity you are likely to encounter on shipboard can probably best be seen by looking over the passenger list on one typical trip: a two-week journey of the *Oceanic* from New York to seven Caribbean islands. Chris Argyris, the Conant professor at Harvard who has written extensively about business organization, and his wife, Renee, who teaches art at Wellesley, were on board. So was five-year-old Effie Saka of Brooklyn, collecting her birthday present from her parents. Edith Cohen, who owns a ready-to-wear business in Ware, Massachusetts, won the cha-cha con-

test. Mr. and Mrs. Manfred Freitag of Larchmont, New York, celebrated their forty-eighth wedding anniversary on board. Emilio and Maryanne Lena Cascio were also celebrating an anniversary: They had met on board the *Oceanic* just a year before.

There was a large Canadian contingent among the passengers; the lure of warm Caribbean waters is especially strong to those spending the rest of the winter in the snowy vastness of Quebec or Ontario or Saskatchewan. The Gilbert Monroes flew to New York from Webster, Missouri, to catch the plane; he's an aeronautical engineer there. The Albert Wetters—mother, father, son, and daughter—took only the first half of the cruise: They got off at Aruba, to go from there to their home in Caracas. From Massachusetts, the Ben Iannouccis and the Lawrence Civettis got on board shortly before the Wetters got off; an unexpected winter snowstorm had blocked roads so badly they did not make it to the Hudson River to catch the ship, so they flew to St. Thomas and joined the cruise there. And Anthony LoRe of Clifton, New Jersey, was taking his wife, Isabelle, on something of a busman's holiday: LoRe is himself a ship captain, master of a cargo ship that sails from eastern U.S. ports to the Mediterranean.

Many of the *Oceanic* passengers had rounded up a group of six or eight friends or family members to travel as a bunch. More formal groups often take cruises together, too. Sometimes the group tour—like the *Fairwind* cruise selected by the Stan/Am club, a Chicago group of annuitants of the Standard Oil Company—is strictly for adventure and relaxation. But sometimes the fun goes hand in hand with business meetings, and you'll

see fellow passengers shuttling from poolside games to serious sessions in rooms reserved just for their conferences. Among the groups that have recently held such meetings at sea are Berkshire Life Insurance Company, the Detroit Bar Association, Lockheed Aircraft, the 3M Company, Honeywell, and the Canadian Jewellers Association.

If you are ever charged with making arrangements for such a meeting, definitely consider a ship as an alternative to the usual resort in the woods. Chances are that there will be fewer complaints about the food and more praise for the ambience than any on-land meeting place you can select.

Ships commonly make available an entire range of audiovisual aids, have facilities for displays if your meeting needs them, and can arrange for anything from a "full charter"—where you bring hundreds of passengers and take over the whole ship—to a meeting for fifteen or twenty. The cruise staff can be talked into throwing a private cocktail party for your group and putting on fashion shows or other "ladies' events" if your group is made up primarily of men and they will want special entertainment for their wives while the meetings are in session.

Eastern Steamship Lines, which puts a lot of its marketing effort into selling the concept of meetings, even assigns a group coordinator to each meeting to provide help, over and above that of the regular staff, in registrations, boarding, luggage handling, and the like. Carnival Cruise, another company that goes after the meeting business, also offers to put together special shore excursions at the ports of call that will feature visits especially tied in with the topic of your meeting or the special interests of the members of your group.

At entirely the other end of the travel spectrum from a large group traveling together is the vacationer on his or her own. Here we can endorse wholeheartedly the suggestion of Georgia Hesse, travel editor of the *San Francisco Sunday Examiner and Chronicle*, that singletons should "consider a cruise. You may set sail on your own," she says, "but by the second day out you'll have had the opportunity to make dozens of friends and acquaintances at your table, in bridge or badminton competition, in the lounge after dinner.

"Cruises are particularly comfortable for older independents, since they relieve you of baggage problems and transportation worries. All you have to do is enjoy, enjoy."

Rosalind Massow agrees. In her book *Now It's Your Turn to Travel* she points out that "loners on long voyages are anything but lonely; cruise directors see to it that there are no wallflowers on any cruise ship. Everyone is importuned to join in the activities, but this is not to say that you can't go off to a shady side of the ship to read a book."

You can, in fact, do virtually anything you want to do, which is why cruising does not attract any particular "type" but every type of person in the traveling world. The simple answer to the question "Who goes on cruises?" is "Everyone."

The Right Cruise for You

4 Timetable for Booking

By now you know enough to know if a cruise is the vacation for you. Or rather, since we're not willing to admit that there is anyone who would not have a good time on a cruise, whether a cruise is the vacation for you this year or next. If not this year—if the need to visit your grandparents or immerse yourself in the art treasures of Italy gets top priority right now—put this book aside until the sea calls you more strongly. But if an outing soon is going to be dedicated to nothing but fun, let's get down to specifics.

Cruise vacations, as we have said, are booming in popularity. It is not unusual for lines to report in September that they are all sold out for some departures in January and February. Every year fall bookings for winter cruises are running 25 or 30 percent ahead of the year before. Until recently, bookings for winter didn't really start in earnest until after Labor Day, but now some lines say their cold-weather departures are half booked by the first weekend in September.

Some of the extra demand has been taken care of by moving to U.S. ports ships that have been sailing in other parts of the world: the new *Festivale* out of Miami, for instance, used to be the *Vaal,* a liner serving South Africa. But as cruising business perks up on other continents, that source is diminishing. And it takes years to build new vessels. "The cruise business has a tremendous growth potential in terms of demand," says William Schanz, president of Paquet French Cruises, "but we don't have that growth potential adding ships."

William Kyle, marketing vice-president for Sitmar Cruises, agrees. "Even with the demand for cruises at an all-time high, ship operators are not rushing to shipyards to build more liners," he says. "The cost of

35

building passenger ships today makes new construction prohibitive, and at the same time the availability of serviceable ships which can be converted for cruising is diminishing."

And, even though winter is still the most popular time for cruising, there really is no slack season anymore. Some lines vary the rates with the season, so while folks who want to get away from northern winters are attracted to January cruises, those looking for bargains scramble for the October departures. Ships that ply the Caribbean in winter are shifted to the increasingly popular Alaska service in summer, or to Mediterranean sailings, or to the Bay of Fundy or the Gulf of Bothnia, so there's now virtually no season in which the available cabins outnumber the passenger demand. And now the lure of African cruising is creating a wintertime alternative to the Caribbean.

That means you have to plan ahead. And if you have strong ideas on which date you want to travel or cabin you want, the need to sign up early is even greater—especially if you have your eyes on the least expensive cabins. They tend to go first.

Line policies vary somewhat, but the "berthing books" generally are opened six months to a year before the sailing date. No individual reservations are filled before that date, although some blocks of cabins may have been put aside for groups or for travel industry "wholesalers" who plan to add other features to the cruise and find customers for the entire package. Travel agents can, however, request individual cabins before the actual bookings begin, and those requests are taken care of as soon as the books are opened, in the order they are received. So if you already know that a cruise on an in-demand ship is how you want to spend the twenty-fifth wedding anniversary that is coming up in two and a half years, it is sensible to get your agent to send a letter off to the line right now.

The need to plan ahead to get the best selection is eased considerably by the fact that it won't cost you anything if you change your mind later. When your reservation is accepted, the line will extend you an "option"; that means they will hold a particular cabin—or, sometimes, simply a promise of a cabin in a defined category—for a week or two, to see if you want it. If you do, you will have to make a deposit at the time, probably about $150 per person, although that, too, varies with the individual company.

The rest of the money is not due until nearer sailing time—typically, six weeks before. Anytime before then that you decide not to take the cruise, you get your full deposit back, no argument. Once you have paid the full fare, you can still pull out and get money back, but there will be some loss, most frequently a flat fee charged by the line for the nuisance of having to find a new customer for the cabin at such a late date. That risk can be eliminated, if it worries you, by taking out cancellation insurance, which guarantees you a full refund if illness or an accident forces you to call off the vacation.

The option from the line is not a take-it-or-leave-it proposition. If you are offered one of the cabins you originally asked for—and the longer the list of acceptable cabins you can proffer, the greater the chances are that you will get one—it would be sort of silly not to take it. But if it is smaller or in a different location than what you like, you can dicker. Chances are that the line thinks it is the best cabin available in the price category you requested, but not everyone's idea of "best" is the same. If you would rather be on a lower deck but nearer the middle of the ship, or have a bigger room without a porthole, tell your agent so and see what he or she can do. And consider whether it is worth it to go up one price category to get something closer to your ideal location.

If the ship is already pretty well booked, the line may offer you not a particular cabin, but a guarantee. They will specify the price, whether the cabin is inside or outside, the deck, and the number of beds, but not the exact cabin. Take the chance. We always feel more comfortable knowing ahead of time exactly which cabin we're going to sail in. But, since it is the lower-priced cabins that go first, very often with only a guarantee you end up with a much more luxurious cabin than you are paying for. The line's specification of the deck and size the cabin will be is only a minimum, and they may give you something a lot snazzier—at no extra cost, of course.

But don't let all this talk about planning ahead dissuade you from acting impulsively, and trying to find a cruise with space for you on short notice. Since accepting an option costs nothing, there are always some travelers who button down a choice cabin and then cancel out a few weeks before sailing time. And often space held for groups or tour packages is more than the demand requires, and those cabins are released to individual passengers as embarkation date nears.

So if the line doesn't have what you want, ask to be put on the standby list and keep your fingers crossed. (Your travel agent should be able to ferret out from the line some indication of how many are ahead of you on the list, which should be a clue to the likelihood of the kind of cabin you want coming through.) And if you win the lottery—or your boss gets so exasperating that you feel you'll explode if you don't get a real vacation immediately—try to find space on a ship leaving soon: You may be lucky.

Almost every departure, in fact, has on board some passengers who just decided to go sailing, and managed to find an opening. Isaac and Rena Ash are one couple that got a last-minute cancellation on a midwinter Home Line cruise and accomplished their packing in one day. On the same voyage were Boston physician Abraham Ginsberg and his wife; they had stepped off a returning cruise liner one Saturday morning, looked at New York City blanketed in snow, and immediately booked a cabin to sail back to the Caribbean that afternoon.

5 How to Rate a Ship

But, of course, the point is not just to find space on any ship, but to find the right cruise for you. The more care you put into making your selection—talking with your travel agent, poring over brochures, talking with friends who have sailed, visiting the ships yourself—the better the chances that you'll tap into the special joys available from a vacation at sea.

And for most of us, the first consideration is cost. While you can spend virtually as much as you could want on a cruise—a veranda room on the *Queen Elizabeth II* can cost $6,000 per person for a ten-day voyage from Los Angeles, and that's not even the most expensive accommodation on board—most people are interested in how little a cruise will cost. It's a good rule of thumb that a moderate double-bed cabin on the outside of the ship (with a porthole) will cost about $125 a day.

There are ways to cut that cost. As we've said, some lines offer lower rates during the spring and fall; you can save about 7.5 percent from peak rates during September and October and perhaps half that in April and May. And some give discounts to special categories of travelers: Chandris Lines, for instance, gives a 15 percent reduction to passengers who book accommodations during January for any time later in the year, a 10 percent discount on some sailings to those over sixty-five, a 10 percent discount to four persons sharing the same cabin, and a 20 percent cut on some cabins to travelers between the ages of eighteen and twenty-five. Younger children sharing a cabin with their parents virtually always get a fare break, often traveling at half or less of what an adult would pay.

On a few older ships—such as the *Britanis* or *Regina Prima*—you can still get cabins without their own baths or toilets. The facilities are only a few steps down the corridor and shared with only a few other passengers. It is a very personal decision how much convenience on that score you are willing to sacrifice, but the money savings can be substantial.

Most ships also have cheaper cabins that do have private facilities, but are (a) inside—with no window or porthole—or (b) very low in the ship or (c) with bunk beds instead of two side-by-side beds, or (d) all three. Experienced cruise customers often opt for these, knowing that they will be spending little time in their cabins and deciding instead to stretch their dollars to more days at sea or more shopping in port or more frequent vacations.

"It's kind of silly to blow a whole vacation bankroll on a bed and bathroom," says "Today" TV show travel editor Stephen Birnbaum, in defense of this take-the-cheapest argument. Rebecca Greer, in her book *How to Live Rich When You're Not,* similarly suggests that sharing a tiny stateroom with others and going "down the hall to the bathroom" is a fine way to husband your vacation money, since one is out of the cabin most of the time anyway.

But, as Ric Widmer, marketing director of Norwegian Caribbean Line, says, "First-timers are reluctant to be at the bottom of the price line or on the lowest passenger deck." Whether that is wise or not depends a lot on personality, but we advise most tyro liner passengers to spring for something in the middle range. The cramped feeling of the smallest cabins can get a trip off on the wrong foot before the fun has had a chance to start. And there's something very nice about watching an approaching island—or even just the lapping blue sea—from the comfort of your own digs. A cruise in the cheapest cabin is infinitely more exciting and relaxing than no cruise at all, but spending a little more can produce a large return in pleasure for each of the extra dollars.

We've been talking about the per day cost. Of course, the longer the cruise, the more the total cost, and a good way to economize without sacrificing luxury is to test the whole vacation-at-sea idea with a short cruise. A three- or four-day jaunt can give you a feel of what it's like. But be warned: You're likely to get hooked.

"For the first-time cruise vacationers, a three- or four-night Bahamas cruise is an eye-opener and usually leads to other longer cruise holidays," says Mort Esterling, senior vice-president of Eastern Steamship Lines, which specializes in short trips on the *Emerald Seas.* "There is time at sea plus time in a foreign port, with the ship right at the dock, to make going and coming easier."

There are a lot of different lines competing with Eastern in short Florida-to-Bahamas cruises on a semiweekly schedule. But you can catch the occasional short cruise from other ports to other destinations, too. Holland America, for instance, usually offers a couple of four- or five-day trips from New York to Bermuda in the spring. There are trips from Montreal down to the mouth of the St. Lawrence and back on oceangoing liners. In Europe, there is a variety of short cruises from Piraeus (Athens) to various Greek islands, or in the Mediterranean from French ports. You can often sign on for just a short portion of a long cruise.

The point is that if you want to see what cruising is like as part of another vacation—or want to go but do not have the money to manage a week-long trip—your travel agent should be able to find some cruise that will fill your special needs.

One option is the "cruise to nowhere"—a seagoing party that usually leaves a big city on Friday night and comes back Monday morning, never having called at another port. It can be a riotous time—nonstop carousing—but won't give you a very accurate feeling of what a "real" cruise is like. The lack of destination does make a difference, and such trips tend to attract a crowd a bit more raffish than your usual cruise selection.

Perhaps the best way to save money is to seek out a ship that is especially geared to the less monied crowd. Russian lines, for instance, know that they don't have the alluring image of Italian fun or British seamanship, so they counter with what have to be considered bargain rates. "Russian ships are priced $100-$200 below competitive lines, depending on cabin category, and there is a no-tipping policy" that adds to the saving, pointed out travel editor Bruce A. Douglas of the Muncie (Indiana) *Star* after a trip on the *Odessa*. Ann Tuckerman of the Christian Science Monitor News Service says unequivocally of a cruise from New Orleans on the *Odessa's* sister ship, the *Kazakhstan*, "We chose this ship for our midwinter vacation primarily because of price. My husband and I paid $428 for a middle-range cabin; the cost of a similar cruise on another line was at least $200 more per person."

World Explorer Cruises is another line that tries to find a special niche in the market by charging less than the going rates. Its summer-only cruises use the *Universe,* which most of the year is run as a student ship, and therefore is less lavish with public space than competing liners of the same size. "We don't pretend it's as luxuriously appointed as some of the other ships around, but it's spacious and comfortable and perfect for the budget traveler," claims Jules Diebenow, an official of the line.

Combination passenger-cargo ships also tend to be cheaper than regular liners, considering the spaciousness and good location of their cabins.

They will not cost less than the least expensive berths on a liner, but they will cost you less than comparable accommodations on an all-passenger vessel. These are not freighters, but ships like the *Santa Magdalena, Santa Maria, Santa Mariana,* and *Santa Mercedes* run by Holiday Inns' Delta Steamship Lines; they carry about one hundred passengers and have a full complement of entertainment for vacationers, but also do an extensive freight business. This means a less precise schedule and more time in port—because sailing times depend on the loading and unloading of cargo—and is a money-saving compromise a lot of travelers like.

You should choose your ship by more than price level, however. Personality is important. Georgia Hesse says that "many passengers overlook this question, although the personality of a ship can be as important as the ability of the crew that mans her. For instance, French ships are famous for their cuisine and *joie de vivre;* Scandinavian ones for spotlessness, modern artworks, and efficiency; Italian ones for conviviality; British for traditionalism."

While all liners offer a wide range of entertainment, check to see how much of it is scheduled after midnight, like the London Pub shows—with lots of audience participation—put on in the wee hours on the *Pacific Princess.* That's a signal that the liner attracts a more energetic, and therefore probably younger, group of travelers. What are the dress rules at lunch, which is the most variable meal? You can always opt to eat at an outdoors buffet and not change out of your swimsuit, but if the line's rules request a coat for men in the dining room at noontime, interpret that as signifying there is likely to be an older, more conservative passenger list.

You can pick up a lot about the personality of a ship and the persons who sail on her by visiting one as she gets ready to leave on a cruise. Saturday is usually the busiest day on the cruise piers in New York, Miami, and Los Angeles, and you can get a chance to look over three or more ships and compare the ambience. Of course, all is bustle and confusion as passengers and well-wishers crowd aboard, but a lot of the oceangoing tone comes through; you'll get a feel of just how casual or precise the operation is, and be able to eyeball the kind of people with whom you would most like to spend a week or two afloat. The fun is infectious, even if you are not seeing anyone off, and it's an easy way to get a minitaste of what a cruise is really like.

And you can count on the steamship companies themselves to be honest about the kind of cruise they are offering. After all, they want repeat business, and know that a poor match between ship and passenger will not produce the optimum vacation memories.

For instance, Robert Dickinson says unequivocally, "As far as Carnival Cruise Lines is concerned, our cruise is not for everybody. It's not for clients looking for luxury and the $150 per day luxury price tag. It's not for clients looking for gourmet dining with flaming dishes prepared tableside. It is not for stuffed shirts or curmudgeons. We're selling the concept of Fun Ships."

Paquet's Bill Schanz is just as frank in comparing two of his ships: "Many potential passengers think of cruise ships as either being too formal or having too many old people. We have tried to combat these misconceptions by offering a choice of cruise style. Aboard the *Azur*, which cruises to the Greek islands, Israel, and Egypt, the way of life is informal and appeals to the young as well as the young at heart. Traditionalists, however, enjoy the more formal style of the *Mermoz* cruises."

You can get objective as well as subjective clues to the mood on board. Birnbaum suggests dividing the ship's gross registered tonnage by the number of passengers to give you "the amount of space available per passenger, and although this is not always a foolproof rule, it is usually true that the higher the ratio of space to passengers, the more comfortable the ship." And, one might add, the more expensive. The *Kungsholm*, now the P&O *Sea Princess*, rates an amazing 56 on long cruises—for which they accept fewer passengers than they do on short voyages—but any rating of 40 or more is a sign that you will never be crowded. Alternatively, the ships with lower ratios will probably be the livelier ones, so you have to choose just how much elbow-rubbing you want.

Tonnage is not a measure of the weight of the ship, but of its size. The "ton" is a unit of measure equal to one hundred cubic feet. A ship actually has a number of tonnage figures: Net registered tonnage measures the space left over after deducting for machine rooms, crew quarters, and the like, deadweight tonnage measures its carrying capacity; displacement tonnage is, roughly, the weight of the ship, since it is the weight of water displaced by the fully loaded ship. But when you are talking about cruise ships, unless one of the other phrases is specifically mentioned, "tonnage" means "gross registered tonnage," or how big the whole ship is.

It is another major factor for you to consider in picking a ship. The biggest liners—with the QE2 heading the list at 66,851 tons—have a superabundance of everything: not just a pool, but probably three to choose from, for instance. They may even offer a choice of dining rooms. Movies will be shown each day in a separate theater, rather than in the lounge used for nightclub shows at other hours. There will be more books in the library, more gifts in the shops, more different activities going on at once, more people among whom to choose new friends.

Does that turn you on or turn you off? It's a matter of taste. Big ships are likely to ride more smoothly than smaller ones, but since most cruising is in calm seas anyway, it's less a plus than it may sound at first. And since big ships often have to dock fairly far out in the harbor at ports of call, they may force you into a longer tender ride to get to your sight-seeing. It's really a judgment call, and the travelers who, on land, think first of the big showplace hotel or the resort with hundreds of rooms and dawn-to-dawn program of sports and entertainment should probably opt for the biggies afloat.

At the other end of the spectrum are the oceangoing equivalents of the small hotel with a wishing well, the side-street hostelry where the concierge knows your name by the second time you enter the lobby. The

Stella Oceanis, for instance, is rated at just 6,000 tons. That makes it rather like a yacht run by a multimillionaire who happens to have 280 friends. It can go places that bigger ships cannot, and can offer an intimacy and personal attention from the entire staff that on a big ship you will receive only from the particular stewards assigned to your cabin and dining room table. But there are certainly fewer different spots to go to, and fewer passengers among whom to find your one special stranger. And smaller ships tend to be noisier.

"The small size of the ship makes the *Oceanis* cruise a different product," admits Jean-Claude Potier, general manager of Marriott Corporation's Sun Line, its owner. And the same is true of other ships in that class. "The average passenger on these cruises will have already cruised at least ten times on a great variety of ships and they know what they are looking for," Potier has found. "It's a small market for a small ship."

Despina Messinesi, who over the years has traveled on, and written about, a variety of liners, is in favor of a middle position: a ship of around 20,000 tons. There, she says, you can get the best compromise of coziness and personal attention and "all the comforts and luxuries that are the *raison d'être* for ship travel."

Until recently, it was important to consider the age of a ship, too. Older ships gave you a much rockier ride, but by now they have been retrofitted with the best stabilizers to counter rough seas, and there's no clear advantage of newer ships over older ones. The cruise business has been so good that ship lines have been able constantly to refurbish interiors, so age doesn't show, except in an occasional art deco wood inlay or frosted glass panel that reminds you of craftsmanship long gone. Most lines put each of their ships into drydock annually to reupholster, repaint, and generally keep things shipshape.

So ships like the *Ellinis* and *Britanis*—built in 1932 to ply between Hawaii and the mainland—look as spanking up-to-date as those built in the 1970s: P&O's *Sun Princess, Island Princess,* or *Pacific Princess,* say, or the Cunard *Countess* and *Princess,* the newest ships in the cruise business. In fact, it is rare for a ship not to have had a previous incarnation: the fifteen-year-old *Doric* sailed as both the *Shalom* and the *Hanseatic;* the *Navarino* used to be the *Gripsholm,* and the popular *Carla C* was the French Line's *Flandre.* Just recently, the *Ithaca* was renamed the *Dolphin* and moved from Aegean cruising to the Miami-to-Bahamas run.

In general, new ships tend to have cabins turned out on the cookie-cutter approach, with a whole deck made up of identical offerings. There are a lot more variations on the older ships, where rooms are fit into all sorts of odd, twisting spaces, and tiny, uninviting cabins can be found right next to showy, large ones: They are from the days when the wealthy traveled with servants cloistered nearby. That means that if the ship you choose was built before the cruising boom took off in the mid-1950s, you have to be a lot more careful about checking the size and configuration of your cabin. On the other hand, if you are looking for bargains, this is where they are to be found, either because you may be able to land a nicer-than-average cabin priced just like smaller adjacent ones, or because you can find, at minimum dollars, the sort of broom-closet accommodations that were left out of the newer ships.

Another thing to look at in selecting your cruise is the enormous range of special-interest sailings that are offered by the lines. If you have any qualms about whether you will find enough to do on shipboard to keep you busy, or whether you will find enough companionable souls among your fellow passengers, a theme voyage should still them. They add to the regular scurry of activities an entire new layer of shows, meetings, and lectures, and ensure that there will be one central interest shared by a majority of the vacationers aboard.

The variety is virtually unlimited. The Theatre Guild each year runs a cruise featuring top actors and actresses. The American Film Institute does the same thing with move stars, lecturers on film history, screenings of classic pictures, and even such special events as auctions of props used by some of the biggest stars. Commodore Cruise Line runs country music festivals on one of its ships, and "Queen of the Ball" cruises on another, with prizes for the best couple in such competitions as the tango, cha-cha, merengue, and waltz. Other lines feature daily concerts by noted classical music performers on some trips.

It's not all show business, of course. Cruises built around bridge lessons and duplicate competitions are frequent; some even feature such famous bridge aces as movie star Omar Sharif. With the growing popularity of backgammon, you can find cruises devoted to that game too.

Another gambit that is growing in popularity among cruise marketing planners is the trip devoted to cooking. Daily lessons in Italian cuisine are available on some Costa Line trips; faithful attendance will even earn you a diploma at the end of the cruise, and a cookbook is included as a free memento. Ed Meyers, executive editor of *Popular Photography* magazine, sometimes gives photography seminars at sea. The Cunard *Princess* usually offers "Health and Fitness" cruises in the pre-Christmas season, which not only feature makeup and exercise lessons, but send you ashore with a free six-month membership in a health spa in your hometown.

More scholarly groups sometimes sign on with a ship line to offer floating seminars. The American Museum of Natural History, for instance, has organized trips that follow the path taken by Charles Darwin in his voyage to the Galapagos Islands on the equator off the coast of Ecuador. The management of the *Stella Oceanis* has teamed up with Rand McNally & Company; the map publisher puts a geographer on each cruise from Puerto Rico who not only gives on-board lectures on the locations along the itinerary, but also leads walking tours at the ports of call.

Learned lecturers are particularly common when the ship is visiting Greek islands or other ports where an understanding of the history will help you enjoy your sightseeing more. For instance, on its cruises stopping at Havana, Carras brings along a professor of Latin American history. The *Royal Viking Sea* employs a University of California oceanologist on its Alaska runs to explain phenomena the ship passes en route.

And not all the instruction is historical or scientific. The *Sunward II* carries professional snorkeling instructors to prepare you to enjoy the fascinating underwater attractions in the clear sea off some of the out-of-the-way Bahama islands at which the ship calls.

Besides such special attractions, size, ambience, and price, a fifth element you will want to consider in picking a cruise is its length. We've pointed out that a voyage of a week or less can be a way to save money and to sample the cruise concept, but that by no means suggests that vacationers who have never been at sea before should spurn longer sailings. Longer trips can give you a better balance of port days of sight-seeing and seagoing days of leisure. They tend to give you a touch more elegance, more time to get to know new friends. They often are the only way to see some of the most exotic and interesting ports of call. And, of course, they give you more of all the good things a cruise offers: Why settle for seven days of bliss if you can have fourteen?

The round-the-world cruises are still the epitome of shipboard elegance, even if they are no longer the domain of the "mink and diamond" crowd. And you can now get a taste of such a voyage without signing on for the entire three-month tour. The *Queen Elizabeth II,* for instance, breaks its globe-girdling annual trip into seven segments, any one of which can be booked separately or in any combination that fits your plans. Get on in Los Angeles, and visit Acapulco, go through the Panama Canal, on to Venezuela, St. Thomas, Florida, and end up thirteen days later in New York. Or take a more offbeat segment, from Capetown, South Africa, to the Seychelles Islands, Bombay, Colombo, and Singapore. An airplane ties every point of embarkation and disembarkation to your hometown. You can also get off at one stop to see a country in detail, then fly on to pick up the ship again a week later at another port.

But do be cautious about signing on for more than three or four weeks straight on a cruise unless you are sure it is the vacation for you. After that length of time at sea, even a lot of vacationers who love shipboard life begin to tire a bit. For instance, a newspaperman interviewed James Hill recently near the end of what was to be a fifty-three-day cruise from Los Angeles. Hill, who had just retired from a job on the docks at Tacoma, had always wanted to see what life was like aboard the ships he loaded. "So now I know, and I'm glad," he said. "It's the most relaxing thing I've ever done in my life. But now I wish it was over."

Here we have been going on for all these pages talking about how to pick the right cruise, and we have yet to mention where the ship is going. Isn't that the most important point of all, the first thing to consider? Well, yes and no.

Larry Zimmerman, a vice-president of Sitmar Cruises, notes that itinerary is usually the decisive question for the first-time cruise customer, and of much less significance to those with more experience at sea. And many other travel industry experts echo that viewpoint. The truth is, it depends a lot on what kind of cruise and which ports you are talking about.

Certainly the general area of a cruise is of prime importance. If what you are seeking is a couple of warm weeks away from winter snows, you're not going to pick an Alaska cruise, no matter how "right" the ship is for you. And if you have your heart set on seeing some of the ruins of ancient civilization on Greek islands you don't care about the features of a ship that is going to Amsterdam, Bergen, Dublin, and Southampton.

On the other hand, although government tourist offices spend millions of dollars to convince you otherwise, there are few passengers for whom the difference between a stop at St. Martin and one at Antigua is going to make the difference between a memorable vacation and a flop. All the lines try to balance their itineraries: a French island and an English one, an island with a lot of historical sights and one with beautiful beaches, a stop for duty-free shopping for luxury imports from around the world and one that features native handicrafts. And, although the names may change, the mix won't end up radically different.

There are, of course, all sorts of exceptions to this ports-don't-matter rule:

• If there is a particular place that you want to look over to see if you would like to spend an entire vacation there.

• If there is a unique attraction or experience that promises to be the high point of the trip for you. Going through the Panama Canal is particularly memorable for a lot of travelers; the new Coral World on St. Thomas is unlike any other tourist show in the world.

• If you have already seen a number of spots in the region, and want not to duplicate your previous travels.

• If a cruise is the easiest way to see a country that either does not welcome tourists with open arms or is short of first-class accommodations. Havana, Leningrad, and Alexandria all fall in this category. So do cities that are fascinating, but where less adventurous travelers would be happy to combine their sight-seeing with the safety and security of their clean shipboard stateroom at night; we put Surabaya, Devil's Island, and Banjul—cruise stops all—in that league.

Besides looking at the stops your ship makes, look very carefully at just when it is scheduled to arrive and depart. Although these are only tentative times, with weather conditions varying the schedule somewhat, if they are not well planned, what looks like a prize itinerary can turn into a real bust. Consider: (a) how long you will have at each stop, (b) when in the day it will be, and (c) what day of the week it will be.

There are, for instance, lovely small islands where the main attractions are isolated beaches and tropical flowers, and a few hours' stay is enough to get a taste of the pleasures. But we are not morning people, and part of our concept of a vacation is lying late in bed. An itinerary such as the *Rotterdam* once posted, arriving at Port-au-Prince, Haiti, at 7:00 A.M. and pulling out again a half hour after noon, isn't going to be awfully attractive to us.

Many passengers on Aegean cruises complain that they do not have enough time to savor the most picturesque islands, especially on schedules that try to work in two islands a day. Some ships stop at Santorin or Hydra for only two hours; we know of one cruise that allotted only two hours for Delos. You can tell the folks back home that you were there, but that's about it.

Sometimes the destinations listed in the colorful brochures put out by the ship lines suggest that you can do a lot more than is possible during a stop. One company, for instance, used to list under its stop at Playa del Carmen in the Yucatán Peninsula both Mayan and Toltec ruins as well as the scuba-diving paradise of Cozumel Island. All are, to be sure, reachable from the port, but given the mere eleven hours of the call, passengers had to pick one attraction or another, and couldn't hope to see it all. Check the hours carefully against the sights you hope to see and their distance from the port.

Most schedules put you in a port during the part of the day when you most want to be there: evenings in spots with nightclubs and gambling casinos, midday for beach resorts. But it pays to check to be sure. The lines tend to be less careful about days of the week, however. On Sundays—and even Saturday afternoon—local shops tend to be closed, particularly on the smaller islands. Those geared to bidding for the Yankee dollar will unshutter when a liner heaves into view, but you will end up with a skewered picture of what local life is really like, and perhaps with shopping aims unfulfilled.

The first port, of course, is the one you leave from. Never before has there been as much choice as there currently is in the cruise market: Port authorities are vying for the significant ship business, and lines are trying to inject excitement into their schedules by adding new ports. New York, Miami/Fort Lauderdale, Montreal, San Francisco, and Los Angeles are still the first North American ports you think of, but they are being joined by occasional embarkations from a host of other oceanfront (and gulf-front) American cities. Boston, Philadelphia, Washington, Norfolk, Charleston, Tampa, New Orleans, Galveston, Seattle, and Tacoma now play host to cruise ships.

Another successful ploy is to make a liner's home port right in the middle of the destination area. At least six lines have ships sailing out of San Juan. Nassau sometimes serves as the departure point for Caribbean circle trips. Acapulco is the origin for some cruises, and Aruba and Curaçao for others.

In Europe, too, more cities are getting into the act. While most Italian cruises left from Genoa or Naples, now some go from Civitavecchia, the port of Rome itself. Ships leave from Toulon in France. Las Palmas, capital of Gran Canaria in the Canary Islands, is now the home port for ships cruising the west coast of Africa. The Holland America *Prinsendam* is berthed in Singapore.

It used to be that cruises had their prime popularity with travelers who lived near ports; the double cost and bother of getting to the port city and then on the ship just seemed too much to many people. So cruise-line marketing managers came up with air/sea packages that cut both the price of getting to the ship and the nuisance of transfers.

The details vary from line to line, but the basic components are a good break on the air fare—either on a charter being flown just for cruise passengers or by a discount from the fare of regularly scheduled airlines—and all arrangements to get you from the airport to the ship. The savings can range upward of half the air fare—and on the longest cruises, the "upward" is significant. One example: Lauro Line gives absolutely free round-trip air passage on Alitalia between New York and Genoa to any passengers taking its fifty-five-day cruise from Italy to South American ports and back again.

The special air/sea prices often include a free night's stay in a hotel in the departure city for passengers arriving from too far away to get there easily on the day of departure. Even for customers from nearer cities, Norwegian Caribbean throws in a free lunch in the Green Dolphin restaurant, overlooking Biscayne Bay, between the airport and the dock in downtown Miami. For economy-minded cruise passengers, Carnival Cruise Lines even offers a special deal on rail fare to Miami.

The flight and cruise can often be coupled with a bargain price at a resort hotel for a few days before or after your sailing. For passengers choosing ship cabins in the upper price range, these hotel stays—at places like Paradise Beach Hotel in Barbados or the Eden Roc in Miami Beach—can be entirely free.

When air/sea packages were first introduced in the mid-1970s, they originated in only a handful of major cities. If you lived in Des Moines, you still had to pay full fare to Chicago to hook up with the special deal. But by now most lines have expanded the arrangement to fifty cities or more; the list varies from ship to ship, but some such arrangement is available from such towns as Bethlehem, Pennsylvania; Dayton, Ohio; Madison, Wisconsin; Little Rock, Arkansas; Greensboro, North Carolina, and yes, Des Moines.

The departure city can offer a minivacation before or after your cruise itself. In New York, for instance, Warren S. Titus, president of Royal Viking Line, says, "People come here for a few days' shopping on their way." In Nassau or San Juan, there can be nights at the gaming tables before or after a cruise. And, of course, a Mediterranean or North Cape cruise can be the perfect relaxation after a couple of weeks of intensive running around the capitals of Europe.

So, to recap, here are the key points to consider in matching up your personality with a vacation at sea:

- Cost, both the per day cost and the total cost of the trip, measured against the kind of comfort you are seeking
- Ambience, atmosphere, affinity with other passengers
- Size of the ship
- Length of the cruise
- Special programs or instructions or competitive events
- Itinerary
- Schedule
- Port of departure

That's a lot to juggle, but only because the cruise lines have such a wide variety of offerings. You can probably walk up to the rack in your travel agent's office that is stuffed with cruise brochures, close your eyes, pick one at random, and be sure it will give you a good time. But we want you to find the trip that will give you the time of your life.

6 The Deck Plan: Chart for a Happy Cruise

In narrowing down your choice of ship, you'll plow through piles of glossy sales brochures, full of tempting pictures. Between the purple prose ("island hopping in the beautiful Caribbean combines the romance of Europe with a throbbing Latin beat") and hyperbole ("here is the epitome of everything a great cruiseliner must be") you will find some useful facts about the ship—size, passenger, capacity, staffing—and the mood of its cruises. But the single most useful peek you can get into what life on a particular liner will be like is the deck plan. Take the time to study it with care.

The deck plan is the road map of the ship, and like those you use to plot car trips, it is full of signs and symbols you have to learn to understand. There's little uniformity, so check the legend in the lower right corner. If you want a cabin with a tub, you won't end up with one with just a shower if you are careful about differentiating the symbols of the two: A little rectangle may be a tub, and a dot with lines radiating from it a shower.

Often the deck plans in the sales brochures will not show the rooms in such detail, but will merely indicate where each number is in the ship. But precise deck plans—showing every piece of furniture—are available, and you can get one by leaning a bit on the line or your travel agent. As we have pointed out, some newer ships have been put together in assembly-line fashion so that, in a given price category, every room is just like every other one. But on older ships there's enough variation to make it worth your while to look cabin by cabin in the area of the ship you have settled on.

The cabins will be relatively small, so much so that only a few companies openly list the dimensions of the rooms. An average two-bed cabin will run between 175 and 200 square feet, including the bathroom. And the cheapest cabins will be smaller than that. Even the most luxurious rooms afloat are tiny in comparison with similar suites at five-star hotels. The new luxury accommodations on the QE2, for instance, that go for a minimum of $1,000 a day and feature sycamore and leather cabinets, Minton china tea sets, and damask bedspreads, measure only 1,000 square feet. That's divided into two bedrooms, two baths, a sitting area, and two terraces, the larger of which is 15 feet by 20 feet and is the largest of the seven separate areas.

The deck plan will always be laid out with the front part of the ship (forward) to your right as you look at the drawing. Do you care whether you sleep lying in the direction you are moving or at right angles to that direction? If so, notice carefully which direction the beds go. Are you planning to travel with lots of clothes? If so, count carefully the number of wardrobes in the cabin; some will have more than others. A bidet? Some cabins will offer one and other won't.

If you envision teaming up with another couple for a card game occasionally in your cabin, you'll want to be sure you have armchairs (which can be moved around a table) rather than a built-in settee. Traveling with another couple, you might (or might not) want cabins that connect. A tiny symbol—perhaps of pair of arrows—will show you which adjoining cabins have a door between them and which do not.

A cabin with a bed that becomes a sofa during the day would be your choice over one with fixed beds if you expect to spend a lot of time in

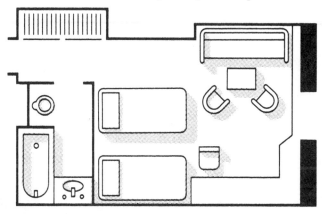

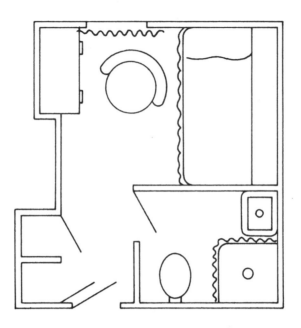

your own quarters reading or relaxing during the day. (On the *Jason,* every cabin converts to a sitting room for daytime use.) If you are traveling with children you intend to have sleep in upper berths in your room, there may be nothing more than a little dot to show you which rooms have foldaway bunks and which do not.

Until recently, ships offered—at least in rooms less expensive than the grandest suites—nothing but single beds. But now you can find a few lines that outfit cabins with double beds; on Norwegian Caribbean Line, the cabins that do have singles are constructed so the two beds can be pushed together to make a double. On the *Festivale,* there are 180 rooms with queen-size beds, and that same pattern will probably be repeated in the new ship the *Festivale*'s owners are now having built.

The particular arrangement of a room may be more or less attractive to you. Long and narrow, or more square? With an entrance foyer, or without? With a porthole or a window, or no outside view at all? Always refer to the deck plan: On some ships, there are cabins on lower decks that are along the outside wall, but nonetheless have no portholes, and therefore are really "inside" cabins.

If you worry about seasickness, you will want a room as near the middle of the ship as possible. And there is less roll on the lower decks, even though they are less fashionable and tend to offer smaller cabins.

Some passengers find walking a strain and want to be near the elevators. Others spurn those locations as noisy and congested. If that rather distinctive smell you get in a beauty parlor bothers you, you wouldn't want a cabin right near the shop.

The point is that you can save yourself unpleasant surprises on board—and turn up little extra goodies—if you invest some time in poring over the deck plan. Even the best travel agent can't really do it for you, because he or she won't know your own likes and dislikes as well as you do. Unless you are booking a year or so in advance, don't pick just one cabin, but come up with a number of alternatives. If none of them is available, the line will offer another cabin in your price range. Go back to your deck plan and check it out before saying okay. If there's a feature about it you do not care for, come up with some other choice of your own. Chances are good that you'll find an available cabin that has the features that are most important to you.

But you study the deck plan for more than just picking your cabin, although we would rate that the most important use. It shows you all the public rooms on the ship, too. All cruises show daily movies, but some have their own cinema, and others show the films in the ballroom (which means, of course, that you can't at the same time pick between a floor show and a flick). The deck plan makes crystal clear just what facilities are there.

The sales brochure is sure to mention how many pools there are on board. But the deck plan will show you if all are true swimming pools, or some are merely wading pools for the small fry. The size of the casino on the deck plan will give you a good clue to how much action to expect there. Similarly, the size of the sports area will tell you whether or not you are likely to have to wait for a turn to play shuffleboard.

Many ships have marvelous little hideaway bars, with just a few seats and the intimate feeling of a neighborhood pub. Spotting such havens first on the deck plan is better than leaving it up to chance to discover them. And if you are on a ship that reserves deck chairs, you can pick out in advance the exact location and deck you want.

None of this is necessary. We emphasize that one of the special joys of a cruise is that you can leave everything up to your travel agent and the line, and not exhaust yourself making a multitude of little, unimportant decisions. But if you enjoy the planning, hours spent with a deck plan can help ensure that your shipboard adventure will be all you want it to be. And as you stroll in your imagination along the glass-enclosed promenade and envision ducking into the Ocean Bar for a heart-to-heart talk with someone special at one of the tables overlooking the moon-bright sea, reading a deck plan can give you, in limited measure, some of the thrill of the cruise itself.

7 That Important Person: Your Travel Agent

Probably the best way to find the right cruise for you—and to get the space you want on board—is to pick the right travel agent to work with. Although you can book directly with the steamship line, you will do much better for yourself going through an agent. As Roberta Ashley, who writes the "Travel Bug" column in *Cosmopolitan,* says, "One of the few legit bargains left in this inflationary world is the travel agent." They won't cost you a cent, because they are paid a commission by the cruise line to handle all the booking arrangements. But that doesn't mean they will be goading you into greater expenses than you want to handle. "A reputable agent won't hustle you into any kind of trip," Ashley assures her readers. "Like your favorite hairdresser, agencies want clients on an ongoing basis and hope you'll recommend them to friends."

They know of sailings and fare deals that have not yet been advertised to the general public, and they can wield clout in a last-minute situation when space is tight that far outpowers what an individual vacationer can muster. In fact, often when the line itself shows a particular cruise as sold out, a good agency will still have some space of its own available.

Here's why: An agency that does a lot of business with a particular ship or family of ships can get an allotment of a particular number of cabins on each sailing during an entire season. If they are not sold to particular customers as the sailing date gets near, they revert to the line's own booking charts. But eight or ten weeks before departure, the cruise headquarters may show a voyage as sold out while some of that allotted space is still available through an agent.

The other side of that story is obvious: Since not all the allotments are used by the agency for every sailing, some of that space will end up in the hands of a line that weeks before had none at all to sell. And since would-be passengers are given options on space that some do not take, this option space also becomes available closer to the beginning of the trip. "We have options turning over until about the last two weeks prior to sailing date," admits Bob Dickinson on the Carnival Line. "The smart agent knows this and they keep trying. But it doesn't really seem fair that it's only some agents who obtain space because of their persistence, while agents who don't know about this lose bookings."

It is a matter of debate within the industry on just what percentage of all the agencies are really knowledgeable when it comes to cruise bookings. But all agree that there are more who do not know this phase of the travel business than who do. So for the traveler considering a cruise, there's a real dilemma: How do you tap into professional expertise if you want to supplement your own study of ships and brochures with the know-how of someone with even more facts at his or her disposal?

The best way, of course, is to use an agency through which someone you know has successfully booked a cruise. But if you have such a glowing recommendation in hand, you probably won't be looking for additional clues to finding a good agency. If you are going to be the first in your crowd to take a cruise, or if those you know who have taken floating vacations do not speak well of their agents, do a little amateur detective work.

The office itself will provide some pretty clear evidence. Cruise lines tend to ship quantities of their brochures only to those outlets that produce business for them, so if there are folders from a variety of different ships on the agency's racks, that's a good indication that they have cruise experience. Window displays or fancy ship models on the counter are an even better sign that this is an agency that sends a lot of customers on cruises.

Cooperative advertising in newspapers, where the ad features a particular ship, but the signature is that of one or two local agencies, can also help point you to knowledgeable outlets: The lines pick up a portion of the tab for such promotion only from their best suppliers.

In general, a big agency is more likely to book a lot of ship passengers and to have space allotted directly from the lines than a small outlet. Certainly any branch of a big national firm like American Express has at least one agent who knows the ship business cold, although in such a large operation you may have to give up something in personalized service. But there are large agencies—especially those with flashy ads featuring low-priced vacations—that are more geared to selling packages than to custom-fitting vacation plans to your particular needs. And there are small agencies that, because of their client mix or the personal interests of the agents, do an amazingly large amount of cruise business.

You don't have to do everything by indirection. Ask. An agency will most often tell you whether or not it does a lot of ship business. And if you do have the bad luck of running into one that is so commission-hungry that it is inclined to exaggerate its expertise, you should be able to see through the pretense after a couple of questions. An agent who tries to steer you away from the idea of a cruise entirely, or who is unable to compare the ambience of one line and another, should be told a polite but firm "Thank you and good-bye."

Asking questions, getting advice, and picking up pamphlets in no way obligates you to a particular agent. If he or she seems concerned about your individual likes and dislikes and has responsive suggestions to make, stick. But if not, keep looking. Once you decide to book space, however, you have a responsibility to keep dealing with that agency until it really proves itself incompetent, and even then you should tell them that you are taking your business elsewhere. It's only fair, since the commission on your booking is the only pay the agency will get for the help it's given you.

Trying to be cute and put two agencies in competition with each other can really boomerang and bollix up your vacation plans. A cruise line will not issue two separate options for the same passenger. The line will advise the two agencies, and while all the monkey business is going on, another agency, working for another client, can grab the space that you had your eye on.

It's obvious but worth saying: The more help you give your agent by describing your life-style and vacation dreams, the more help he or she can be in putting you together with the right ship. Unless you are working on a very short deadline, the agent should not expect you to make up your mind to book at the first conversation. That session should be for narrowing down the alternatives, and you should go home with sales material for two or three different cruises that seem to fit your specifications. Experienced travel agents will know the questions to ask about time, money, and what you want out of your holiday to narrow down the possibilities, but the more advance thought you have given to the matter, the better the relationship will work.

8 A Packing Checklist

One of the changes the new casual tone has brought to shipboard life is that there is a lot more ease in dressing than in the days when, on carefully planned evenings, women simply *had* to wear long gowns and men without dinner jackets, although admitted to the dining room, were definitely made to feel that they weren't keeping up their end of things.

There are fewer musts now, and if you are the kind of traveler who likes to squeeze a week's worth of dressing out of a single suitcase, you can do it.

But why? The air of elegance is one of the special things a cruise ship offers in today's world, and we would argue to all but the most dedicated of the blue-jeans crowd that this is the time to put on the dog. The clever little outfits that can be dressed up or down with a snap-in dickey or a collar that can convert from open sport shirt to dress wear are essential when you are trying to hit six European countries with luggage you have to wrestle into an airport every second day. On a ship, with the ability to unpack only once for the whole vacation and to have plenty of closet and drawer room, why not take as many complete changes as you like. For many women, sweeping into the dining room every night in a different outfit can be the highlight of a trip, and a cruise is the one chance to do it all.

Basically, you need three sorts of clothes for the cruise: shipboard day wear (which can be no more than a swimsuit, coverup, and sandals, if you want to live by the pool), evening wear, and clothes to wear sight-seeing at the ports of call. The third category is the one that cruise passengers most often overlook, bringing down on themselves embarrassing stares when they tromp into the downtown of a foreign capital wearing halters or Bermuda shorts. Few tropical islands follow a life-style requiring dark suits or day dresses, but they do have codes of behavior that are a lot more structured than some Americans seem to think. You may not play tennis on Bermuda courts, for instance, unless you are outfitted entirely in regulation whites. Plan to dress the way you would sight-seeing on an August day in a major U.S. city, and you'll look just fine.

The clothes will obviously have to be suited to the kind of weather you are cruising in—summery for the Caribbean, but warm enough to stave off the chill night winds on a cruise to Alaska or through the Norwegian fjords. And you will need more variety on a cruise that starts in one region and plys to another—Los Angeles to Alaska, or New York to Puerto Rico—than an Aegean or Mediterranean go-round that stays in the same climate zone.

"The best rule is to wear what you would find suitable for a country club," says Frances Koltun in a good one-sentence summing up. She points out that since ships "are splendid floating resorts, your clothes should be casual and *sportif* by day, pretty and romantic by night."

There's no need to buy anything special for the cruise, but if you do, "it is slightly ridiculous to overdo the marine theme and dress like a member of the crew with embroidered anchors, brass buttons, and an officer's cap," warns Genevieve Antoine Dariaux, former *directrice* of the Nina Ricci fashion house in Paris.

She does suggest, however, that cruisewear is one category where you can opt for brighter colors than you might pick for the streets of Cleveland or Salt Lake City. "Stripes and bright, clear colors such as blue, turquoise, orange, coral, red, and yellow are always attractive on board a ship," she advises. And that advice applies to men's wardrobes as well as women's: *Saturday Review* travel editor Horace Sutton describes the scene at the captain's cocktail party on a recent trip: "Dress was announced as 'formal,' a pronouncement that drew dazzling raiment out of

the traveling wardrobes of the passengers. A paisley dinner jacket; a canary-colored jacket worn with white turtleneck, white flannels, and white plastic loafers; an evening dress made of one enormous mola, a creation of the Panamanian San Blas Indians, were among the choice ensembles."

Basically, it's a question of deciding what personality you are wearing for these days at sea, and then choosing the clothes that best show you off the way you want to be shown off. But here's a checklist, not so much to pack by as to plan by. It's a middle-of-the-road list that can be pared down considerably by the most frugal packer, and expanded by those who revel in their finest feathers.

For Women

Plan to board wearing a smart daytime outfit, a two-piece dress or suit and blouse, high-heeled shoes, and carrying a capacious pocketbook. Put in your luggage:

- ☐ 2 long gowns
- ☐ 1 long skirt
- ☐ 2 dressy tops (chiffon blouse or beaded sweater, for instance) to go with the long skirt
- ☐ 1 short dressy dress
- ☐ 4 or 5 T-shirts or cotton shirts (including some with long sleeves)
- ☐ 2 pair shorts
- ☐ 2 sport skirts (or more if you don't wear shorts)
- ☐ 2 cotton dresses (or coordinated separates)
- ☐ 1 pair slacks
- ☐ 1 pantsuit
- ☐ 2 swimsuits
- ☐ 1 swimsuit coverup
- ☐ 1 pair sneakers or espadrilles
- ☐ 1 pair sandals or scuffs
- ☐ 2 pair good walking shoes
- ☐ 1 or 2 pair dressy evening shoes
- ☐ 1 fancy cardigan or evening wrap
- ☐ 1 raincoat (ideally, one that folds up into its own pouch)

☐ 4 scarves (big enough to go over your hairdo)
☐ 1 small pocketbook (to carry essentials around the ship)
☐ 1 evening bag
☐ Sun hat or visor (essential in the tropic sun)
☐ Sunglasses
☐ Wig (if you wear one)
☐ Jewelry, hair ornaments, belts, and your other favorite accessories
☐ Cosmetics and toiletries
☐ 1 robe
☐ Slippers
☐ 2 nightgowns
☐ 7 days' worth of lingerie and hose

For Men

Wear a relatively conservative sport coat (tweed, if you have one light-weight enough) and slacks, dress shirt and tie, and dress shoes to board. Put in your luggage:

☐ 1 dinner jacket and pants (if you have both a black and a light-colored summer dinner jacket, bring both)
☐ 1 dark suit (or 2 if you decide not to bring a dinner jacket)
☐ 1 sport coat (this can be gaudier than the one you wore at embarkation)
☐ 2 pair dress slacks (make one white, if you have them)
☐ 1 pair casual slacks or jeans
☐ 1 pair shorts
☐ 4 dress shirts (including a formal shirt, if you have one)
☐ 4 sport shirts or knit shirts
☐ Ties (including a black bow tie for formal wear)
☐ 2 swimsuits
☐ 1 swimsuit coverup or cabana-set top
☐ 1 pair sandals or scuffs
☐ 1 pair sneakers
☐ 1 pair stout walking shoes
☐ 1 sweater or light parka

- ☐ 1 raincoat (folded into its own pouch)
- ☐ Golfing hat or visor (even if you don't usually wear one)
- ☐ Sunglasses
- ☐ Cuff links, studs, tie tack, etc.
- ☐ Toiletries
- ☐ 1 robe
- ☐ Slippers
- ☐ 2 pair pajamas
- ☐ 7 pair socks (3 sport, 4 dress)
- ☐ 7 sets of underwear

That's a rundown for a seven-day cruise, but for ten or fourteen nights at sea, you won't need much more. Since passengers do not usually dress formally on nights of days when they have been visiting a port, a cruise with fewer stops will present more opportunities to wear formal wear than we have envisioned here, but black tie and long dresses are never mandatory.

Obviously you'll have to put your wardrobe together with some eye toward color coordination. If a man is going to have only one pair of dress shoes, he'll want them to be black to go with his formal wear, and then probably won't want to pack brown sport coats. A woman can wear a sequined top with a pantsuit and make it a zingy evening outfit, but not if the top is fuchsia and the pantsuit orange. Particularly if you are going to travel lighter than our checklist suggests, make sure the various tops and bottoms mix well to give you the greatest number of different outfits.

In addition to the clothes, be sure to include the gear that make a vacation special for you. A camera and all the paraphernalia. Field glasses to pick out sea gulls and dolphins. The latest best-seller or the classic you've always wanted to read, which you can't be sure will be in the ship's own library. Fins and diving mask. Your address book so you can send exotic postcards to the stay-at-homes.

What about electrical appliances, like your razor, blow dryer, and travel iron? The policy and the electric current vary so from ship to ship that you'll just have to check that out with the line or your travel agent. There are almost always some provisions for razors, even if you have to borrow a current adapter aboard. Relatively few lines have provisions to use heavier appliances in the cabins, but a few do, and a few others have special outlets in certain rooms so that you can, for instance, use an iron in the laundry room but not in your cabin.

If you are taking abroad any relatively new, expensive foreign-made merchandise, you should register it ahead of time with the U.S. Customs Service. That can be done at any Customs office, or right at the pier before boarding if there's no Customs office in your hometown. It's a simple operation, but the card you get showing that you owned the item before leaving the country can forestall a lot of trouble if an inspector questions it on reentering. Cameras are the items most often registered, but if you have an expensive foreign-made watch, get a slip for it, too. Don't worry about imported clothes.

Pack everything in sturdy luggage. Unless you are departing on a long cruise, you'll probably not arrive at the pier with a steamer trunk, but stevedores handle all luggage very roughly. Soft-sided suitcases are okay, but only if they are really strong; actually, any luggage that withstands the baggage handling of the airlines will get onto a cruise ship and off again just fine. The porters will not, however, accept clothes on hangers covered merely with plastic clothes bags. If you have a favorite gown you want to carry this way, you will have to tote it aboard yourself.

You will probably be acquiring presents along the way, so be sure there is room in your luggage to bring back more than you took. The best idea is to bring along a tote that folds or zips into the size of a briefcase, and then expands into a full-size weekend bag. If you use this extra luggage for all your purchases, it's likely to speed your way through customs when you get home.

You will also want some kind of little gym bag or tote to carry ashore at the various ports of call. This is particularly useful at stops where your main desire is to enjoy the surf and a tropical beach, but even on sightseeing stops you will be happy to have a convenient bag to carry purchases or the sweater that you wanted in the early-morning air but that became too hot as the day warmed up. Depending on the kind of totes you own, of course, this can be the same bag you take along for carrying purchases home.

Many ships have coin-operated laundries on board, but for most of us a big part of a vacation is not having to worry about such problems as getting clothes clean and pressed. Your cabin steward or stewardess will be able to handle at least emergency clothes care for you—removing a food stain, or pressing pants that got rumpled in an afternoon downpour in port—but you can probably manage on any trip of two weeks or less to take along enough changes so that laundry chores are at a minimum.

The fabrics you choose can make clothes care a lot easier. Lace and chiffon, for evening clothes, pack well and tend not to crease. The same is true of knits; synthetics, of course, are the best, although they may be uncomfortably hot in truly tropical climes; cotton-synthetic blends or all-cotton fabrics treated to drip-dry are a better bet. And men should be sure to include some all-cotton socks for island sight-seeing; the nylon type just doesn't absorb perspiration well enough.

And the atmosphere itself (using the word literally) helps in easing the clothes-care burden. As Mary Scott Welch wrote in *The Seventeen Guide to Travel*, "Going by sea, you'll find that the damp air is almost as good as a steam iron."

9   Getting There and Getting Going

Loading a ship and pulling out on a cruise—often less than twelve hours after the ship has arrived in its home port from its previous journey—is a mammoth operation. Even with practiced efficiency (and the line that doesn't manage that doesn't stay in business) there's inevitably an air of bustle that borders on tumult. The trick for the passenger is to have things arranged well enough so that you move through all the proceedings in your own little oasis of serenity. You want the bustle to add to the excitement of departure on a fabulous voyage, but not to become a hassle.

Those arriving at the port as part of an air/sea package have it made. Representatives of the line or the packagers will meet you at the airport, take care of your luggage, and whisk you to the ship. Or to lunch and then to the ship. Or to your hotel for the night, meeting you there the next morning to take you to the ship. In any event, all you have to do is be there; everything else is arranged for you.

But if you are getting to the pier under your own steam, do plan on arriving early. Usually embarkation extends over a three-hour period. If there are some extenuating circumstances—infirmities, say, or an infant in your party—your travel agent may be able to set up special permission for you to board before the rest of the passengers. But otherwise, try to arrive about a half hour after embarkation begins. That way you will miss the backup of the early birds, but still be ahead of most of the crowd. And you'll get to settle in and make whatever arrangements you have to on the ship more quickly. It also provides more time for partying.

Coming by cab, of course, leaves you no problems. If a friend is driving you, all the major ports have plenty of space for visitor parking. If you are driving to the port yourself—a big plus when you get back from your trip and want your own wheels right there—whether or not it is a problem depends on the city from which your cruise leaves. In the United States, for instance, there's ample parking right at the pier in both major Florida ports, Miami and Port Everglades, and New York City, which used to present a parking nightmare, now has a great long-term parking garage. Have your travel agent reserve you space there. In Los Angeles, there's shuttle bus service to the pier from a nearby garage. In San Francisco, there's no system at all: You just find whatever space you can (it won't be near the dock) and cab it from the garage. The cruise lines will be honest with you about the facilities in other cities; generally, though, ports that handle only an occasional passenger ship have loads of room to leave cars during your cruise.

At any U.S. port, all you have to do is get your luggage to the entrance to the pier. Stevedores take over there, and you won't see your bags again until they are delivered to your cabin. There's usually so much commotion that it's hard to have faith that the system is going to work, but believe us, it does. The regulations say not to tip the porters, but we wouldn't leave all of the possessions we need to make the trip a joy in the hands of one of those guys without adding a five-dollar bill.

Such help is scarce at some foreign ports; our most recent reports from Italy suggest that stevedores are as rare as genuine Masaccios. If you have spent the night before embarkation in a good hotel, try to get a bellboy from there to bring your luggage and get it on board. Otherwise, have along some sort of carrier or set of wheels to make it easy to get your baggage around the pier.

Be sure not to pack your cruise tickets. It's the sort of thing that doesn't just happen in reruns of "I Love Lucy." You will also have gotten from the line forms issued by U.S. immigration authorities, which you should have filled out before you arrive at the dock. Have them and your tickets readily accessible when you get to the pier. On most cruises that is all the documentation you will need for boarding, but if there are other formalities—some South American countries require a passport from U.S. and Canadian citizens—both your travel agent and the steamship line will have let you know well in advance. Often the necessary papers, such as a Mexican tourist card, can actually be issued by your travel agent or the cruise company itself.

Buddies who have come to see you off will board the ship through a separate gangway. The policy varies from line to line and port to port (the Russians, for instance, seldom welcome nonpassengers aboard), but most cruise managers have generous provisions for visitors. They see the frenzied good cheer of departure parties as one of the best sales tools around. More than one of our friends have decided on vacations at sea primarily because of the fun they sensed at a good-bye party in our cabin.

Some lines actually include visitor passes in the information packet they send you with your tickets. At other ports, boarding tickets are sold at a nominal price—with some of the take going to seamen's charities—so

the curious can board and look around, whether they are seeing a friend off or not. Even at spots where security precautions force the lines to limit boarding to passengers, your friends can stand at the pier alongside the ship and you can wave to them over the deck rail.

But if you can, it's certainly fun to get the vacation going with a bon voyage party aboard with some of the folks who are staying behind. It can be an intimate affair or a big blast. If you know that there are going to be a lot of friends and relatives showing up it's best to plan ahead. Have your travel agent make provisions for some hors d'oeuvres to be served in your cabin. It varies from line to line whether there is a charge for these snacks, but when there is, it is minimal: A whole tray of tea sandwiches costs five dollars on the *Rotterdam,* for instance. Your cabin steward will provide ice and glasses free for the asking.

You can have champagne or drinks served, too, but because the ship is still in port and the cabinets full of duty-free liquor are still locked up tight, charges will be relatively expensive. Better to bring a couple of bottles of your favorite brand along for the party, or be sure that some of the bon voyage gifts friends bring will be of the liquid sort.

If you're expecting more well-wishers than your cabin will hold, there's no problem. Just have your travel agent arrange in advance for a corner in one of the public rooms to be set aside for you. The ship will gladly reserve a section for as many guests as you expect, and a lounge waiter will provide the same services your cabin steward will. If the crowd you intended to contain in your cabin overflows, put through a hurried call to the office of the hotel manager, and he can probably find some unassigned space to give you for the party.

But you may take your leave of land without a gaggle of friends around, either because you are sailing from a port city far from home, or because you and a companion choose to make it a very personal moment. That needn't make it any less festive. Follow the advice of novelist Carole Chester: "If you don't want friends to see you off amid popping corks, wave to everyone on the dock anyhow and retreat to your cabin for your private celebration as the tugs start leading the ship from the wayside."

Fun on Board Guaranteed

10 Make Yourself at Home

It's an exciting moment when you walk up the gangplank and a seaman offers you a hand to step on board. This floating hotel is going to be your home for the next few days or weeks. To enjoy it fully, get to know it. We've talked with cruise passengers who discovered on their last day at sea a delightful little cocktail bar they never knew was there, or a shop that had just the gift they spent hours of port time searching for. Don't let it happen to you: Locate yourself, and discover all the wonders the ship has available.

In the entrance hall where you board, a cadre of crewmen will be lined up. One will take your hand luggage and lead you to your cabin. If your steward there has studied the passenger list enough ahead of time to address you by name immediately, you'll know you've drawn a real gem.

The room will be smaller than you expected. That's part of the reality of ships. Designer Mary McFadden warns that "almost any ship's cabin will seem confined when you first arrive," but she says the space is usually so well designed that "you quickly learn to live in it." The cabin will also be sparkling and inviting; flowers or bon voyage gifts sent by friends or your travel agent may already be in place on the dressing table. On Norwegian America Line, the company puts a bottle of champagne and a basket of fruit in every cabin as a welcome-aboard greeting.

Don't settle in, but go at once to take care of a couple of chores that can have a lot to do with how much fun you have the rest of the voyage. The first is getting your table assignment in the dining room. You are given one spot, and unless your unhappiness with the location or your companions leads you to ask for a change, that is where you will have every dinner and most lunches. (Breakfast customers are seated at the next

75

open table on some ships, although others ask passengers to use their regular tables for the morning meal, too.)

On the more elegant ships, your travel agent can forward your preferences when you book your ticket, and you will find in your cabin a card with your specific table location. But on most lines, you have to hie yourself to the dining room lobby, and wait in line for your turn before the maître d' and his big chart. Even so, it is best if the travel agent has passed on the sitting and kind of table you want.

Most ships do not have a dining room big enough to seat all the passengers at once, so you have to decide whether you want to eat a bit earlier than you would really like, or a bit later. Once you've made the choice, you've made it for all meals for the whole voyage: You can't take an early lunch and late dinner. But let dinnertime really make up your mind, because there are alternatives—breakfast in bed, buffet lunches at poolside—for the other meals. So the key choice is between dinner at around 6:30 and dinner at around 8:30; that is really the one "appointment" on your cruise where you have to be reasonably prompt.

The other key choice is what kind of table. On many voyages, there are more requests for tables for two than the maître d' can fill. If you are honeymooning or you and your companion are in a honeymoon mood, be insistent about wanting to be by yourselves. But sharing a dining room table is the very best way to meet your fellow voyagers and to strike up new friendships, so don't shy away from the bigger tables. Certainly anyone traveling alone should opt for a table for eight. Tell the maître d' what you would like in the way of dining company, and he'll put to use his years of expertise at matching passengers.

We would advise, though, staying away from tables for four, unless all are traveling alone. If you and your companion get stuck with another couple who are less than scintillating, it can dampen the considerable joy of mealtime afloat, while a larger table gives more chance for diversity, and for diluting one dullard. If you're taking the trip with another couple, of course, then that's an exception to our rule, and a table for four is just what you should ask for.

It used to be that the next stop after getting your table assignment was getting your deck chair. But now many ships do not assign deck chairs, but simply provide them free, for you to pick as the sun and your desires change. Your travel agent should have told you what the policy is on your ship. If the chairs are assigned-and-charged-for, you can decide if you want to be where there is maximum sun or under the protection of a covered part of the deck, and whether you prefer the boisterous fun of being near a pool or a quieter spot farther away. If you change your mind, the deck steward can always move your chair as the fancy strikes.

McFadden says, "The first thing I do when we board the ship is head for the hairdresser to make shampoo appointments every three days for the whole cruise. Also arrange for manicures, pedicure, and time in the exercise room." Other travelers want to schedule massages right away, or plan a private session with the golf or tennis pro who is often a member of the cruise staff. But these usually can be done by telephone from your cabin.

Now you can reward yourself for all that diligent planning and start the bon voyage festivities. As Elizabeth Post, editor of the Emily Post etiquette books, notes, the bustle of a departing ocean liner is "a fine excuse for a party, and a happy beginning to your trip."

Then kick off your shoes, put your clothes in the drawers and closets and your toiletries in the medicine cabinets in the bathroom. In other words, make your room *your* room. And continue to follow Carole Chester's routine: "When you've unpacked," she says, "use the first few hours of a cruise for orientation. Find out where the public lounges, library, cinema, restaurants, bars, pool, and sauna are." You don't want to be a stranger in this wonderful waterborne resort.

Compulsive travelers will have studied the deck plans carefully ahead of time and charted the way from their cabin to the dining room, the pool, and the sun deck. But if you haven't boned up in advance, at strategic points on each deck—next to the elevators, for instance—there will be posted big schematics of the ship's profile, showing which public rooms are on which decks, and the layout of the deck you are on.

Sometimes these take careful reading, since you cannot always reach one part of a deck from another by just walking along an aisle. All cruises are one-class affairs, so there are no gates separating the turf of one class of passengers from another, as there used to be on transatlantic liners. But still much of your ship is given over to quarters for crew and officers, and those areas are off limits to passengers except by the most special invitation. So to get from where you are to where you want to be, you may have to ride down two levels, walk the length of the ship, and then ride up two levels.

It used to be that ships designated the central deck as "Main" and counted down from there: A, B, C, and even D on some of the biggies. Above Main often came "Upper" and then perhaps "Promenade." But since the lower decks have less cachet, the lines began disguising them with names instead of letters, although often keeping the same pattern. The *Dolphin,* recently put in service between Miami and the Bahamas, for instance, calls its cabin decks Atlantis, Barbizon, Caravelle, and Dixie. On other ships, however, not even that pattern holds, and the style of naming the decks varies greatly from one ship to the next.

There are, however, certain consistencies that will help you find your way on most ships. The majority have a Promenade deck which will feature walkways running the entire circumference of the ship; often those amidships are covered, with big picture windows looking out to sea. This deck, or the one immediately above it or below it, is likely to be completely devoted to public rooms, with gathering places small and large, often quite impressive ones: The grand salon of the *Mermoz* is brightened by a ceiling containing three thousand lights.

The Boat deck is the one where the lifeboats are carried, and will be above the one with the bulk of the public areas. A sports or sun deck will be even higher, offering the optimum place to get a tan and the most active games, such as deck tennis or miniature golf.

These levels are always called *decks* on a ship, never floors. And the same thing goes for the actual flooring. Sailors will speak of going *above* or *below* rather than up or down. The front of the ship is the *bow* and the direction you walk to get to it is *forward;* the back of the vessel is the *stern,* and you get there by going *aft.* Those nautical terms have permeated enough of landlocked life so it's not very hard to get used to them; you'll soon understand a steward who tells you that the place you have asked about is "two decks below, aft."

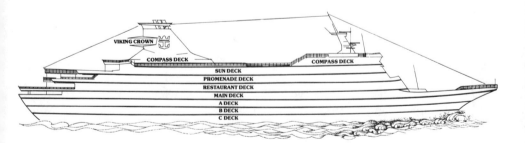

But lots of landlubbers have trouble with *port* (left) and *starboard* (right). A strong prejudice against the heavy fortified wine the English so relish has led us to remember which is which by following the rule that, regardless of the occasion, port is never right; serve if it you wish, but no one will want it, so it is always left. But if you like the drink, you'll have to work out another mnemonic device of your own.

Port is a more recent coinage than *starboard* and was picked precisely because it sounds so different from the name for the right side. Mariners used to the word *larboard* for the left side, and the possibilities for confusion abounded. Both *starboard* and *larboard* are themselves corruptions of words for the main oars that were used to steer ships in the days before rudders. The vessel was directed by a long ore mounted aft on the right side, which originally, because of its function, was called a *steer board*. To keep down sidewise drift on ships with a shallow draft, a compensating board was then added on the other side. That side, the farther from the wind, was known as the *lee side,* just as the Virgin Islands, Montserrat, and Nevis are now known as the Leeward Islands. With time, the board on the lee side came to be called the *larboard.*

Today the port side of the ship is always indicated by a red navigational light, and markings to emergency exits on that side are also usually in red; green lights and arrows are used on the starboard side.

And, by the way, the conveyance in which you are traveling is always referred to as a *ship.* A *boat* is a vessel carried on board a ship, such as the lifeboats or tenders used to carry passengers into port.

Here's a rundown of other nautical terms you'll encounter on your cruise, and the names for some of the special shipboard features that you will notice and wonder what to call. Don't worry about mastering it; officers and crew will understand you perfectly well if you mention a "flag" instead of *colors* or call it "that thing the rope is wound around" instead of a *bitt*—but use it as a reference, and if you can add a new word or two to your vocabulary, it will help underscore that a liner, like a foreign country, is a place quite distinct from home.

> ABEAM. At right angle to a line running from the ship's bow to its stern.
> ACCOMMODATION LADDER. A folding stairway that can be swung out from the gangway to a tender riding on the sea.
> ALLEYWAY. A passageway.

ALOFT. Above the highest deck.

AMIDSHIPS. In the center part of the vessel.

ATHWART. Abeam; running from the port to starboard side of the ship.

BACKWASH. Water trailing the ship, thrown back by the propeller.

BAR. Shoal or sandbank.

BATTEN DOWN. Make an area—most often the cargo hold—absolutely watertight.

BEAM. Width of the ship at it widest point.

BEARING. Direction.

BELLS. Rung to designate the time, according to the ship system which divided the day into six four-hour periods, with a bell struck for each half hour (three bells could be 1:30, 5:30, or 9:30).

BILGE. Where the ship's sides join the bottom.

BINNACLE. The brass stand that holds the navigational compass.

BITTS. The two short posts on deck used for fastening the line mooring the ship to a pier.

BOLLARD. The post on a pier used for fastening the line mooring the ship.

BOXING THE COMPASS. Naming each of the thirty-two points of the compass in rotation.

BRIDGE. The glass-front office at the forward end of the ship, from which the steering is done and the entire vessel commanded.

BRIGHTWORK. The shining accent points on a ship, usually the brass but also used for highly polished wood.

BULKHEAD. Wall.

BULWARK. The part of a ship's side that extends above the deck, to provide a solid chest-high wall instead of a rail.

CABLE LENGTH. 100 fathoms, one-tenth of a nautical mile, roughly 600 feet.

CAPSTAN. The drum, turned by the windlass, used to raise the anchor and bring in mooring line.

COAMING. Raised molding around a hatch or other opening in the deck.

COLORS. Flag showing the ship's nationality.

COMPANIONWAY. Connecting space between the decks (also refers to the ladder in the space).

CONNING. Steering.

CROW'S NEST. Lookout platform high on the forward mast.

DAVIT. The crane used to swing lifeboats out over the water and lower or raise them.

DEADLIGHT. Steel covering clamped over portholes in rough sea.

DOLDRUMS. The virtually breezeless oceans around the equator.

DRAFT. The shallowest water the ship can pass through without scraping the bottom.

EVEN KEEL. When the ship is perfectly upright.

FALLING GLASS. Dropping barometric pressure, which could be a signal a storm is on the way.

FATHOM. Six feet.

FENDER. Protective material on the side of a ship to keep it from rubbing against the deck; often only old tires.

FLOTSAM. Things floating in the sea from the wreckage of a ship.

FORECASTLE. The section of the ship set aside for the crew (pronounced "folks'll" as in, "Folks'll tell you to go back to your own part of the ship.").

GALLEY. Kitchen.

GANGWAY. Opening in the railing or bulwark through which passengers board the ship.

GUNWALE. Upper part of a ship's side (pronounced "gunnel").

HATCH. Opening in the deck, and also the covering over that opening.

HAWSE PIPES. Holes in the bow into which the anchors are set.

HAWSER. A large-diameter rope or cable.

HEAD. Toilet.

HELM. Steering equipment; both the wheel itself and the post to which it is attached.

HOLD. Below decks cargo storage area.

HORSE LATITUDES. Just beyond the trade winds, where breezes are erratic and infrequent.

HULL. Frame of a ship, without the superstructure.

INBOARD. Toward the center of the vessel.

JACOB'S LADDER. Rope ladder with wooden steps, used to bring a pilot on board.

JETSAM. Things floating in the sea that were deliberately thrown overboard to lighten a ship's load.

KEEL. Thick steel plate running the length of the ship's bottom, to which the main frame is attached.

KING POST. Thick post on deck, to which a boom is attached.

KNOT. One nautical mile per hour.

LANDFALL. First sighting of land.

LEAGUE. Three nautical miles.

LOG. Official record of the daily activities of the voyage.

MACKEREL SKY. Sky full of fluffy clouds, riding high.

MANIFEST. A record for customs agents of all the cargo on board a ship.

MOOR. To anchor.

NAUTICAL MILE. 6,080 feet (15 percent longer than the mile measurement used on land).

OUTBOARD. Toward the sides of the ship; the opposite of *inboard*.

OUT OF TRIM. Not properly loaded, so not sailing on an even keel.

OVERHANG. Portion of stern or bow that juts beyond the hull.

PELORUS. A navigational device.

PITCH. Motion of a ship from stern to stern.

PLIMSOLL MARK. A circular mark painted on the side of a ship which shows how heavily the vessel can be loaded in various sea conditions.

POOP DECK. Partial deck aft, one level above the main deck.

PROW. The part of the bow that rides above the water.

QUAY. A simple wharf, often just a paved bank (pronounced "key").

RIGGING. The ropes and chains that support the masts.

RISING GLASS. Rising barometric pressure, indicating pleasant weather ahead.

ROLL. Motion of a ship from side to side.

RUDDER. The metal fin at the stern, used to steer the ship.

RUNNING LIGHTS. The basic, required nighttime safety lights to warn other vessels of your presence.

SAMSON POST. A less frequently used name for a king post.

SCREW. Propeller.

SCUPPER. Small hole below the rail so deck water can drain off.

SCUTTLEBUTT. Originally, a cask containing drinkable water; now, any shipboard drinking fountain and, by extension, the kind of gossip passed on over the water cooler.

SIDELIGHTS. Part of the complement of running lights, red on port and green on starboard.

SOUNDING. Water depth.

STEERAGEWAY. The slowest speed at which the rudder is effective in steering the ship.

STEM. Forwardmost part of the ship.

SWELL. Long series of waves.

TAFFRAIL. The rail around the stern of the ship.

TRADE WINDS. Those winds blowing from a westerly direction toward the equator.

UNDER WAY. Anchor up and ready to go.

WAKE. Trail left in the sea by your ship.

WATER LINE. Fine line painted on the side indicating ideal portion of ship to be submerged.

WEATHER SIDE. The side of the ship toward which the wind is blowing.

WEIGH. Lift (as in "weigh anchor").

WINCH. Engine and drum used to weigh anchor, handle cargo, lower lifeboats.

WINDLASS. Particularly powerful winch.

WINDWARD. Toward the wind.

YAW. To go off the established course.

11 Who's Who on Board

Myra Waldo, the food and travel writer who spends a staggering 60 percent of her year away from home seeking out new recipes and new vacation havens, laments the fact that "many of the old courtesies and gracious details that once made traveling a pleasure have fallen victim to what we like to think of as progress." But the one general exception to this rule, she says, the one place where a high standard is still set for personal service, is aboard ship.

That's not accidental. "Cruise ships are one of the last refuges of a staff that nurtures a pride in service," claims Ralph Hartl, director of Hellenic Mediterranean Lines. "The cruise passenger is treated as a person, not a number or member of the group."

We agree wholeheartedly. There may be a few havens left where the traveler can find the same level of attentiveness—the finest hotels in London or Lisbon, the most exclusive Swiss resorts—but they are priced so that only society's select will ever cross their doorways. Cruises are luxury for everyman.

Attentiveness is to a large extent the result of an attitude. But it has its quantitative side as well, since the helpers with the best will in the world can't do the job if too many tasks are thrown at them. To get a rough idea of just how much you can expect of the staff on your ship, do a simple calculation: Divide the number of passengers carried by the size of the whole crew. A ratio of one crew member per two passengers promises an indulgent voyage, and some liners better that: On the *Sagafjord*, the formula works out to one crew person for every 1.4 passengers, even when the ship is filled to capacity.

But as willing as the shipboard staff will be, they can't read your mind. And, being made up of humans, more than one member you will encounter will be just lazy enough not to want to do more than he or she must. That means you have to ask. The limitation on the service available is only your ability to think of things you want. Being waited on hand and foot is all included in the price of your tickets, so don't hesitate. If the crew and staff didn't genuinely enjoy giving service, they probably would have taken up another line of work. But you often have to give them the clue.

That means you have to know just who is who aboard ship, and what responsibilities go with each title.

The big cheese, of course, is the captain, and he will be nothing at all like Merrill Stubing, as portrayed by Gavin McLeod on ABC-TV's "The Love Boat." Some are austere and some are jolly—we still cherish the memory of a Sun Line captain who vigorously led a round of challenging Greek folk dancing—but all have years of exemplary service under their belts and radiate an air of command. No indecisiveness in a liner master. He's in complete charge of the ship, with the same kind of responsibilities as—and a lot more authority than—the mayor of a good-size town. His word is law.

Nearly a hundred years ago, Mark Twain wrote: "The Cunard people would not take Noah himself until they had worked him through all the lower grades and tried him for ten years. It takes them about fifteen years to manufacture a Captain, but when they have him manufactured to suit at last, they have full confidence in him." And in the years since, little has happened to outdate that observation.

Captains to a man have worked their way up to their exalted positions through many steps. The career of Giovanni Ruffini, master of the *Oceanic,* is typical. He started as a maritime apprentice at age fourteen, where he juggled seagoing duties with a continuation of his school studies. He graduated from both the marine commerce course at the University of Naples and the Leghorn Naval School, and took tours in the Italian navy and the merchant marine before turning to passenger ships. He got his first command, of the *Argentina,* in 1949, and served as captain of three other liners before taking the helm of his present ship.

The number two in command, the captain's deputy, is usually called the staff captain. Their immediate subordinates are in what is called the Deck department of the ship.

The next largest group of officers is in the Engine department, and is headed by the chief engineer. Power is his domain—not the kind wielded by the captain, but the kind that moves your floating pleasure dome through the ocean waves. He's directly in charge of the engine room, with a ranking of first, second, and third officers under him. Also important on the chief engineer's staff will the chief electrician, in charge, as you would guess, of the entire shipboard electrical system.

The chief radio officer directs a separate staff, which in in charge of radio communications. He's the ship's contact with the rest of the world. News bulletins, sports results, stock market closing prices are gathered by his network and either posted on a special bulletin board on deck or included in a daily newspaper slipped under each cabin door.

One of the joys of ship travel is the sense of being cut off from everyday cares, but if you need personal communication with the rest of the world, it's available. That, too, is the responsibility of the chief radio officer. Check with his office either to send a written message (a radiogram, but usually called a cable) or to make a telephone call. Calls go out only for a portion of each hour, but the radio-room staff will have you paged when your connection is made. Voice quality is spotty, but generally adequate. Due to international law, there's no shipboard phone service, however, while the ship is in port or within fifty miles of land.

If a radiogram comes in for you, it will be delivered directly to your cabin; a paging system will summon you for a telephone call. (Regular mail can be sent to you at each port of call in care of the cruise line's agents; you'll have gotten the specific addresses when you received your tickets.)

The duties of the medical officer (now often merely called the doctor) are the same as they would be on land, but he, too, has officer rank.

These are all personal titles, which the officers carry with them on duty or off. But there are other titles that are passed from man to man, depending on who is in charge at any given moment. If the captain is not on the bridge, for instance, the officer to whom he has delegated his authority over the ship is called the Officer of the Deck. And his counterpart in the engine room, the officer temporarily wearing the mantle of the chief engineer, is designated the Officer of the Watch.

All of these officers have very specific, technical jobs to do. If you are allowed onto the bridge or down into the engine room and have questions to ask, they will probably be happy to explain operations to you, but only if they have time. Pick your moments and consider yourself lucky if they can give you some time; don't be insulted if they are too busy for you at any particular time.

But ships do expect officers to fulfill social duties as well, particularly the junior officers. Despite what you have seen in old movies, they will not be hosting favored tables in the dining room. But they will be on hand for parties, and have some obligation to see that unattached ladies at dances have a fair number of turns around the floor. Contacts made at these social functions are the best way to get a private invitation to see the behind-the-scenes workings of the ship. One exception to that rule: On Russian ships, as Ann Tuckerman of the Christian Science Monitor News Service discovered, "Officers kept strictly to themselves."

But another whole group of officers is directly in charge of keeping passengers happy. The top man on this team used to called the chief purser. Today the officer with that title is usually in charge of finances, cabin assignments, and information on the liner; the overall director of the passenger areas and activities is dubbed the hotel manager. Such officials as the food and beverage manager, chief steward, and cruise director report to him, and he should be your court of last resort if you have an annoyance that lesser lights have been unable to remove.

Ships don't make it as easy as they might to know just which of these august personages is which, because there's no standardization of epaulet insignia. The austere British put four narrow gold stripes on the shoulder of the man in charge of the largest ship now sailing—markings less impressive than third-level officers from countries that revel more in decoration. But whatever the number or width of stripes, the captain will be the man with more than any other officer. On many lines, the engineering officers will have a small three-blade propeller incorporated into their emblem, and the radio officers will show jagged lightning beams enamating from a central circle, rather like the old symbol for RKO motion pictures. The hotel manager may not wear a uniform at all, but be decked out in a business suit to emphasize that his concern is the civilian side of the cruise. Some lines include in the handbook given all boarding passengers a spread showing which insignia go with which titles; if you get one, spend a couple of minutes studying it.

When you talk to the captain, you call him just that: "Captain." You can add his last name to the title, but it's not necessary. Other officers, talking among themselves, may at times refer to the captain as "Skipper," but it would not be appropriate for you to use that title. Other officers can perfectly properly be called simply "Mr. Soandso."

The fact is, however, that when you meet the captain—receiving guests at a cocktail party, say—you'll probably have a chance for only brief chitchat. And the pleasure of your journey will depend a lot more on personnel at the other end of the rankings.

The most important single crew member will be your cabin steward or stewardess. On some large ships, he will be assisted by a cabin boy; sometimes a steward and stewardess will split responsibilities for a cabin, particularly if it is priced in the luxury categories. One of them will be in sight in the hall outside your cabin, or in calling distance, virtually all the time.

It's not really easy to define what a steward does. To begin with, he serves the same function as a maid at a hotel: He makes the beds, changes the towels, keeps the cabin clean. Without your asking, he'll change the water keeping your bon voyage flowers fresh. But unlike a hotel maid, he will not visit your room just once a day, but will keep it in order seemingly constantly. One passenger on a recent voyage on the *Queen Elizabeth II* was puzzled at the way her cabin was tidied up every time she left. "How did the steward know I was out if he hadn't seen me leave?"

she wondered. The trick of the trade turned out to little shreds of paper tucked into each door jamb of an occupied cabin: They dropped on the deck when the door was opened.

But a steward's role goes far beyond mere tidying. He'll bring you breakfast on a tray, and—even when the ship's rules don't allow for it— can usually snare you fresh fruit or sandwiches if you want a snack in the cabin. If you come down with *mal de mer,* he'll have Dramamine available, as well as homey advice on the folk treatment he's found works best. He'll bring you a softer pillow, or a firmer one. He'll take your dirty clothes to the ship's laundry and bring them back clean, and, if you don't have a stewardess, he'll find one to do hand washing and ironing of items too delicate to trust to machines. He'll have favorite spots to recommend at ports of call.

He will look after young children if they are bedded down while their parents go dancing, and pass messages back and forth among members of a family who are going their separate ways. He'll stand guard if you particularly do not want to be disturbed in your cabin, and can even locate an empty cabin for you if such circumstance arises.

When you want to give a little predinner cocktail party in your cabin for new-made friends, he's the one to discuss it with. He'll see to it that there are canapés, glasses, and ice, and that your bar is stocked as you wish.

But those are just the listed functions. His job is really to take care of all your creature comforts. Need a safety pin or writing paper? Just ask your steward. Cabin too hot or too cold? Your steward will make the adjustment. Stewards on Norwegian America liners show up with robes for your trips to the swimming pool. Anything to provide you with a feeling of well-being in his territory.

You, in turn, should let him know that you appreciate his efforts. Of course always say "Please" and "Thank you." But beyond that, get to know him. Ask about his family back home, ooh and aah over photographs if he shows them. You don't have to feel it is somehow beneath the proper station of a passenger to get that friendly with "the help." And

besides making it all the more likely that your steward will make that extra little effort for you, you can tap into a fascinating store of ship lore that he has picked up in what may be most of a lifetime spent on the high seas.

The more special favors you ask of your steward, of course, the bigger should be your tip to him at journey's end. But if you sense he thinks your special requests are taking too much of his time away from other passengers, it would be wise to give him that extra five or ten dollars right then. We particularly recommend some tipping in advance if you are traveling with children or know that you will need special service because of a health condition.

On the other hand, if you run into one of those rare occurrences where your steward from the start is more grudging than the paragon we have described, take the matter up with the chief cabin steward. If he can't get the steward to shape up—and everyone has off days—he may even arrange with the purser to have you moved to another cabin.

When you leave your cabin deck and enter the dining room, a whole new crew of minions takes charge of your welfare. "During the course of the first meal," advises frequent ship traveler James Villas, "learn the names of your dining captain, wine steward, and waiters, any one of whom can make or break your trip, depending on the type of initial relationship you establish." He also suggests that you "take ten minutes at the very beginning to discuss the condition of wines with the sommelier. (Even with the highly sophisticated stabilizers on today's ships, certain French Burgundies and Bordeaux still don't travel too well.)"

The captain oversees a group of waiters, and may recommend special sauces or salad dressing, which he will prepare at tableside. Next up the ladder is the maître d' (or majordomo), who's in charge of the entire dining room. We've much more to say about the importance of these stalwarts to your good vacation in our chapter on food and drink.

On deck there will be a deck steward. His jobs are more limited than the cabin steward's, but the role is the same: to keep you happy while lounging in your deck chair. That can mean bringing you midmorning bouillon or a cool drink, turning your chair toward the sun or away from it, supplying you with a lap robe if the breezes are too chilling.

The fourth group of attendants are those specifically charged with running programs to entertain you. The cruise director is the top man of this

group, and he will have working for him a variety of instructors, sports pros, hostesses, and even nannies. They often come from a show business background; on one ship the cruise director is a former saxophonist with Tex Beneke and his assistants include a PR woman who used to be a flamenco dancer, a former Junior Miss from Massachusetts, an Australian former boy actor, and a couple whose faces are familiar because of the number of bit parts they have played in television commercials. And that show biz training means they are particularly outgoing and professionally anxious to please.

They arrange all sorts of games, parties, and tournaments. But they are also there to put together the unscheduled activity that would be the high point of the trip for you. Just ask. And as Ralph Michele, a cruise director for Italian Lines in its heyday, says, "Don't keep complaints to yourself. Come to your cruise director or his assistants immediately with them. They will be remedied if humanly possible."

12 Keeping Everything Shipshape

From the moment you board the ship until the moment you disembark, your time is your own. Show up for meals or sleep through them, take every class offered or spurn them all. But there is one must, and on some lines it comes soon after boarding, when you have barely begun to find your way around the ship. It is the boat drill. Among all the merriment of shipboard life, safety is the one subject that is not open for joking. Take the boat drill very seriously. Even if your line does not, as Holland America does, actually take attendance, it is foolhardy to skip this one drill.

If the boat drill is scheduled for immediately after departure—on Royal Caribbean ships it comes just fifteen minutes after the ship lifts anchor—your cabin steward will make sure you know. It will also be announced in a daily listing of activities that you will find in your cabin. Never is the drill later than twenty-four hours after sailing.

Basically, the boat drill is like fire drill in your school days, a dry run so that should an unlikely emergency occur, you will know just what to do and where to go, and can respond calmly. The signal for the start of the drill is seven short blasts on the ship's whistle followed by one long one—an alarm that can be heard in every corner of the ship. The announcement will also be made on the ship's internal radio system; on some liners, the system is set up so that emergency messages come through even if the set is turned off. When the signal comes, put on the life jacket that you will find stowed in your cabin, and go immediately to the lifeboat station assigned to your particular cabin area.

The ship carries enough lifeboats so that there is a place for every passenger and crew member. Crew members are in charge of each boat and, in fact, have probably been lowered to sea in that boat just before embarkation time to make sure that all is in working order. Your job is just to know which boat has been assigned to your party.

There will be full instructions in your cabin, and stewards and officers standing in the passageways to guide you along to the proper location. Take the stairs, not the elevators. Don't run, but do be expeditious about it. Even though everyone has to wait until the laggards find the right place, you should be out of your life jackets and back in your cabin within a half hour.

As important as the boat drill is, chances are remote that you will ever have to use the knowledge you pick up there. Modern navigational devices and exacting ship construction standards mean that modern ships are an extremely safe way to travel. In 1960, all the major nations welcoming liners to their ports got together and came up with international rules for Safety of Life at Sea. For any ship calling at a U.S. port, those standards are mandatory, enforced by the Coast Guard. A 1966 Fire Safety Convention laid down even stiffer regulations on the use of flame-retardant materials and watertight doors that can shut off one section of a deck from the rest of the ship.

Ships that travel in the summer in Europe and in the winter in the Caribbean are usually under Coast Guard scrutiny too, since they are likely to call at Miami, St. Thomas, or San Juan or Ponce in Puerto Rico. But standards set by ship insurance companies are only marginally less tough than those of the Coast Guard, and even a vessel that never touches a U.S. port is almost sure to be supersafe. Have your travel agent check into the safety features only if you are booking onto an obscure ship overseas run by a line that is not a member of the Cruise Lines International Association.

There are stringent standards for sanitation as well as safety on liners calling at U.S. ports. Since 1970, the Center for Disease Control of the U.S. Public Health Service has been inspecting ship cleanliness. The current inspection form, adopted in 1976, contains a tough scoring system: If a ship fails to meet even one of the thirty-two most important standards—involving checking literally hundreds of items, such as the precise temperature in all refrigerators—it fails the inspection. The CDC does not have the power the Coast Guard does to stop an unsanitary ship from sailing, but officials there have told congressional hearings that they do not need such muscle. "The industry has been cooperative in accepting our recommendations and guidelines," testified William Foege, CDC director. The main aim of the program—reducing outbreaks of gastrointestinal disease—has clearly been achieved: Although there are far more cruise departures now than a decade ago, such health problems occur no more often than once a quarter.

"There is no small city in the United States where all phases of life are as well organized or as well protected as on a cruise ship, " says Mario Vespa of Home Lines. "The cruise industry is healthy and the lines are actively cooperating with Public Health codes." Although unsanitary conditions on the *America* made headlines in mid-1978, when management inexperienced in the cruise business briefly tried to run the ship, Vespa insists that "with vessels that are normally known to the U.S. public and sail from U.S. ports, it's seldom that they don't meet standards. If an infraction occurs, it's usually corrected before the ship sails."

Norwegian America Line hires sanitation consultants to sail on some cruises and make recommendations for improved procedures. Holland

America now has on every crew a sanitation officer, with a degree in public health or a related discipline. Adds one Cunard executive: "As a result of these inspections, our people on board the ships are much more vigilant and that is all to the good. A ship lives on its reputation."

Under the U.S. Freedom of Information Act, the inspection reports on all ships are available to all comers. Just write, specifying which ships interest you, to the CDC Quarantine Division, Room 107, 1015 North America Way, Miami, Florida 33132.

Health and safety regulations are slated to get even tougher in the years ahead. For instance, by 1980, all ships will have to have improved sewage treatment systems. To meet that requirement, the *Skyward* has already put in a two-tank setup that takes all waste generated on the ship and turns it into a disinfected dust of dry particles. That is then turned into water, chlorinated until it has no harmful bacteria in it, and pumped overboard.

Each passenger has his or her own important contribution to make to health and safety aboard. The greatest fear is a fire at sea; that's why so much of the safety program is devoted to being able to isolate a burning area and keep a conflagration from spreading. But it goes without saying that it is even better to keep a fire from starting, and that requires extreme care with all smoking materials. Do not succumb to the temptation to pitch a glowing cigarette into the dark night sea: A breeze can catch it, blow it back onto another deck, and present the possibility of a smoldering ember starting a blaze. Obviously, too, do not grind out butts on the deck or the carpeting of your cabin: Ashtrays will be plentiful. And do *not* smoke in bed.

You, of course, have a role in ensuring your personal safety as well. If the sea is choppy, use the handrails in the corridors and along the ship side of the open decks. On stairways too. A sudden pitch could send you sprawling, and no one wants to acquire bruises on a vacation.

Use other sensible precautions. At the pool, for instance, never dive in: The rocking of a ship makes that a dangerous move. And stay away from the parts of the ship that are off limits to passengers. One former crew member tells of the time four passengers—all drunk—decided to climb the radar mast. They stumbled over barriers put on the sports deck especially to keep them where they belonged, and climbed the ladder to the crow's nest. There they played a kind of tag game with the slowly re-

volving arms of the radar. What they didn't realize is that each arm is alive with 6,000 volts of electricity and could have knocked them dead on the spot. Foolishness.

What about that dramatic moment you've seen in old movies or new TV shows when the call goes out: "Man overboard." Well, unless you are bent on self-destruction, it's just not going to happen. The railings are at least waist high for a tall person, and there's virtually no contingency in which you could slip in such a way that you would fall over one. The only even remotely likely scenario we can envision for needing a life pre- server tossed to you in the ocean is one in which you had so much to drink that you lost all good sense, wandered to an empty part of a deck, hoisted yourself up into a sitting position on the railing, lost your balance and tumbled from there. If that possibility worries you, be sure to have a watchful friend around after the third drink.

13 So Much to Do

Aboard ship, you're going to be able to live the hour-by-hour life that you want to live. Catch the matchless rosy luster of dawn at sea either on your way to bed or as you get up early for a morning jog around the nearly empty Promenade deck. The sea and the sun and a corps of willing servants are there to let you laze away the days in pampered in- dolence, but if your batteries are all charged up, the cruise director and his staff will have laid on virtually unlimited activities among which to choose.

"Ships are like self-sufficient towns," says longtime liner executive George Reis. "They offer boutiques, a beauty salon, dance classes, tennis, golf, swimming, libraries, a theater, a broadcasting station, and even a neighborhood pub."

In fact, virtually all offer a choice of neighborhood pubs. Perhaps the most unusual is the unique feature of the sister ships *Nordic Prince, Sun Viking,* and *Song of Norway:* a semicircular lounge stuck halfway up the funnel, offering, as you sip, an unparalleled view of the horizon from the equivalent of ten stories above the sea. But every ship lets you move your drinking from intimate little corner spots to big elegant cocktail lounges to pulsating discos as the clock and your mood change. On the *Mardi Gras,* for instance, the range is from The Den, with a packed capacity of 50, to the Grand Ballroom that easily seats 550 passengers.

And your mood will change. Mary McFadden, who turns out expensive hand-painted clothes and jewelry for the couture trade, takes a cruise the middle of every summer to get away from what she calls the "frantic kind of creativity found in a Seventh Avenue factory." It's a time for rejuvenating. "I sleep the first few days," she says, "perhaps from the motion of the ship but probably just to catch up. Then I start on my own therapeutic routine." It includes two visits a day to the gym, jogging at dawn around the deck, and swims in one of the ship's pools.

The theme of this entire book is that the central charm of a cruise is that you can follow whatever regimen you want. But let us encourage you at least to give some of the organized activities a go. Certainly sign on for the trips to the business side of the ship that is otherwise out of bounds for passengers: the bridge, or a tour of the kitchen facilities. This gives you insights into the really awesome complexity of the place in which you are roaming the seas. And try one of the classes or get-togethers; if the event has collected only the more boring or gruesome of your fellow passengers, you can beat a hasty retreat easily enough. But if you never give it a try, you'll never know, and some of the organized fun really is fun, even for those who hate being organized.

The captain's cocktail party is another event that you really should make. One etiquette book still on sale in 1978 gave you the form to follow for writing a formal regret, which it advises you send with a cabin boy if you are going to miss the party. But the fact is with today's more casual shipboard protocol, you are committing no faux pas if you simply do not show up. Truth is, with so many passengers invited, the captain really won't miss you. But you'll miss a social high point of the trip, a chance to learn firsthand from officers about the workings of the ship, to meet some fellow passengers you have not come across otherwise, and to see everyone in their finest finery.

Later in the trip, you may well get invited to other parties organized by the crew for special groups. A cocktail party for those who have sailed with the line before is customary; the repeat customers are especially prized, because the ship's salesmen use their numbers as evidence of how well they please their passengers. Another frequent event is a grand-mothers' tea party; if that's your bag, be sure to bring along pictures of the offspring, because passing them around to appropriate ooh's and aah's is the major entertainment at such events.

The activities listed for one Sunday on the *Sun Viking* as it sailed be-tween Miami and Ocho Rios provide a typical selection. They include a morning exercise class; Ping-Pong, ringtoss, and shuffleboard tourna-ments; dance lessons; a tour of the bridge; an introductory lecture on Ja-maica; a demonstration of how to carve fancy ice centerpieces; a card party; two separate showings of two brand-new movies; a cocktail party hosted by the captain; dancing to live music from 8:00 P.M. "until the wee hours" in one salon while professional entertainers put on a lively variety show in another.

Winners in the various tournaments get shiny trophies. But remember, there's never a hint of a charge for any of it.

Because this was Sunday, there was an interdenominational religious service as well; on cruises in southern Europe, it is common for there to be daily masses.

For activists who don't like group endeavors, there is, quite apart from the tournaments, plenty of space for individual deck games; the equip-ment is there for the asking. For more sedentary competition, the cruise staff will help put you together with other enthusiasts of chess, Scrabble, or backgammon. And from 9:00 in the morning until 6:00 at night, the sauna is open.

Other ships offer other sports. Many have well-equipped gyms, with weight-lifting equipment and exercise machines. Skeet shooting is an-other popular sport. Every cruise ship has at least one swimming pool, and the *Statendam* and *Rotterdam* are among those leaving from New York that offer indoor pools for the northern days of your trip and out-door pools for the sunnier southern days. The *Oceanic* has its unique Magrodome, which covers the entire pool deck when the weather is cool and then opens to let the sun shine in during balmier days. On the Cunard *Countess* and *Princess*, the cruise staff strings a tennis practice net just aft of the funnel, and offers lessons from a tennis pro who is part of the traveling band of experts to guarantee that you have a good time.

Pitch-and-putt courses are sometimes set up on deck, and there may be "driving ranges" that offer golf fanatics something special: an opportunity to slam a ball as far as they can into the bottomless depths of the sea. The shipboard pros can be some of the great names in their sports; the golf expert on the *Oceanic,* for instance, is "Lighthorse" Harry Cooper, who was the leading money winner on the PGA tour back in 1937, the second year he won the Canadian Open.

Two sports, although played elsewhere, are particularly traditional for shipboard fun, and it would be a shame to steam into home port without having given them a whirl. One, of course, is shuffleboard, which combines the precision placement of bowling with the croquetlike pleasure of being able to blast your opponent out of his or her own precision placement. The other special shipboard game is deck tennis, which uses neither racquets nor balls. It does, however, have a net, across which teams toss an O-shaped black rubber coil. The side that fails to catch and return the ring loses the point.

Circumnavigating the deck is another way to keep the muscles toned and can be adapted for any level of vigor from a rapid jog to a saunter. On the *Royal Viking Sky,* six times around equals a mile, and you can get a similar measure for your vessel.

Language lessons are popular on ships with non-English-speaking crews. Passengers on such Russian ships as the *Odessa* and the *Kazakhstan* seem especially proud of the useful phrases they pick up in such classes. Of course, if you have picked a special-interest cruise built around cooking or photography or bridge, there will be daily classes and lectures tied to that theme, in addition to all the regular activities. A recent one-week sailing to the Caribbean put together by the American

Film Institute included showings of ten classic movies, some introduced by scholars or by their directors, others commented on by stars like Olivia de Havilland and Howard Keel.

A lot of passengers like to shop while on the ship. "Sometimes the on-board boutiques have better buys than those ashore," says travel editor Georgia Hesse. They tend to feature the best gift items from the country under whose flag the ship sails, as well as a sampling of the kind of crafts offered at your ports of call. Some even have honest-to-goodness one-day sales, just like the department stores back home. The shops on the *Rotterdam*, for instance, have been known on certain days to sell the Seiko quartz watches in stock for 15 percent off the price tag, or to drop the price of a Waterford crystal decanter from $72 to $59.95.

Also available: cigarettes and liquor sold in bond and delivered to you as you disembark; even with the toll of inflation while this book is being printed, chances are that the cigarettes will be in the ship stores for about $4.00 a carton. Buy five cartons of the same brand, and they may come packed in a free shoulder bag. Some brands of booze that you will probably find going for under $5.00 a fifth include Myers dark rum, Tanqueray

or Beefeater gin, Smirnoff vodka, Black & White Scotch, and Seagram's 7. Luxury items like French cognacs are similar bargains. But check the latest customs regulations before you buy.

It needn't be go-go-go. Ships offer quiet spots, too. The library is the source of a wide variety of reading material (with a distinct bias toward current best-sellers and popular novels of years gone by) that can be borrowed free for the duration of the trip. But it also is a haven of solitude. The writing room will be another such spot where silence is the rule and you can keep a journal or catch up on correspondence in amiable surroundings. Free supplies of elegant engraved stationery and picture postcards of the ship should be stocked in the writing desks there.

And the spell of the passing seascape can provide hours of fascinating entertainment for those who will take the time to notice. It never stays the same: One moment as smooth and glassy as the surface of a mirror, the next it is full of rippling waves. Flying fish and porpoises leap above the sea to play for the watchful.

The sunset is like an implosion, for it falls suddenly off the horizon, and night palpably closes in. The sunset gives off a marvelous range of colors, and golden rays like kindergartners draw on their pictures of the sun but adults seldom see. Later, the stars glow in greater numbers, and from far-ther away, than viewers on land, with the competition of man-made lights, ever have a chance to see.

Bingo is offered most evenings on most ships. Many still follow the old tradition of running "horse races" where you can bet on which wooden nag's head will be first across a finish line; they are moved toward their destination, by liveried cabin boys, according to the roll of a die. On the *Sun Viking,* this particular "sport" has been modernized: Films of actual horse races are shown, with bets placed by passengers who do not know the outcome. Holland America puts on frog races as betting events on some of its cruises. And, would you believe it, the Norwegian America Line has actually been known to run marbles contests.

Not all the gambling is quite so childlike. Increasingly, ships are build-ing in regular casinos, where at least blackjack, if not roulette, is expertly run. Almost needless to say, any expenses you run up on this kind of en-tertainment is not included in your ticket price.

Some evenings will be set aside for costume events: funny-hat contests, say, or a parade of passengers decked out in pirate togs. If it's not your cup of tea, no one will pressure you to join in. But it's a wonderful way to meet new people, both at the costume-making session the cruise staff will hold in the afternoon and again in the grand showing at night. A com-ment on the originality of your costume provides the perfect opening for a stranger who has been debating for three days how to start a conversation.

Some passengers make a big thing of the costume events, even bringing along in their luggage a couple of pieces of clothing especially for dress up. Parisian fashion magnate Genevieve Dariaux says she always takes along some of her mother's clothes from the 1920s. They make a hit at the costume party, and save her "being dressed like everyone else as Ma-hatma Gandhi, draped in a bed sheet with a bath towel wrapped around your head."

Cruise director Colin Hillary has recently been putting together some-thing quite different on the *Rotterdam:* a Dutch country fair. Booth after booth is set up, with a shooting gallery and other games of skill and chance, and even a photo shop where you can put your head through a cutout of a painted life-size figure and come away with a picture of your-self as a wooden-shoed Dutch boy or girl. A ticket booth sells tickets for a

quarter each, and they're good at all the attractions, just like at a real country fair.

The entertainment events put on by the ship staff is apt to include quite lavish reviews staged by the stewards and sailors, revealing talents you hardly suspect when you see them going about their daily duties. One will turn out to be a whiz on the accordion, and another a proficient juggler. But these crew festivals lean most heavily on folk dancing, often with elaborate costumes complementing the dances of the crew's homeland—Italy or Greece or, in the case of Holland America, Indonesia.

The crew entertainers, however, are only a change of pace from all the small band of professional entertainers you can count on seeing on all cruises; often, a singer, a magician, and a dance team. Some quite stylish entertainers who have never quite hit the big time make a career out of entertaining aboard ship. Comedian Joey Villa, for instance, has fashioned most of his routine around cruise jokes. "Food is fantastic aboard ship," he says, "but passengers won't admit to gaining weight. They say the salt air shrinks their clothes." Other Villa stories:

• I said to a woman passenger, "Isn't this a good cruise? We have slot machines, the sun is always shining, there's food every ten minutes, a beautiful swimming pool." She said, "Oh yes—but take away the ship and what have you got?"

• One passenger lost her husband's entire wardrobe. She thought the portholes in her cabin were the washer and dryer.

• I asked a lady up on deck, "Could you go out and see if it's raining?" And she looked at me and said, "Why don't you bring the captain in and see if he's wet?"

On most ships, the same entertainers will perform a number of nights, varying the routine and the costumes. But the *Sun Viking, Nordic Prince,* and *Song of Norway*—all owned by the same line—guarantee different acts every evening. They manage by pooling their entertainers and transferring them from ship to ship at common ports of call.

One of the newest trends in making cruises more special than ever is to sign on really big-name entertainment, particularly during the spring and fall season, when demand for vacations at sea falls off a bit. On a single

recent sailing of the *Daphne,* for instance, blues fans were entertained by Roberta Flack, Dizzy Gillespie, "Fatha" Hines, Lionel Hampton, and Joe Williams. A classical music cruise on the *Mermoz* included among the performers pianists Byron Janis and Peter Serkin, sopranos Marilyn Horne and Grace Bumbry, and Stuttgart Ballet stars Marcia Haydee and John Cragun.

Other music, theater, and literary celebrities offered up on one recent cruise or another include, in alphabetical order, Edie Adms, Lauren Bacall, Art Buchwald, Cab Calloway, Peter Duchin, Philippe Entremont, Joan Fontaine, Stan Getz, Van Johnson, Sammy Kaye, Tony Martin, Zubin Mehta, Anna Moffo, Patrice Munsel, Anthony Perkins, Lynn Redgrave, Joan Rivers, Irwin Shaw, George Shearing, Maureen Stapleton, Enzo Stuarti, and Margaret Whiting. On shipboard, of course, you get an opportunity not only to hear the celebrities perform, but to chat with them at cocktail time or while gazing over the rail at the endless sea.

Paquet started featuring top classical music artists on one annual sailing back in 1961. Today Holland America, Cunard, and Carras are the leaders in putting such name entertainers into their ship shows. Sitmar is trying a different tack: full stagings of such popular Broadway shows as *Hello, Dolly!, Guys and Dolls, South Pacific,* and the Neil Simon comedies *Barefoot in the Park* and *Odd Couple. Royal Viking Sea,* on one recent cruise, even put on *Merry Widow* and *La Traviata.*

The cruise staff will go to great effort to make sure you know what shows and activities are available. You should, for instance, get a guide to the ship as soon as you board, packed with such diverse and useful facts as the telephone number of the ship's doctor, the hours for meals, lapel markings of the ship's officers, and the price of cigarettes in the on-board stores.

The key information source is a daily bulletin that will be slipped under your cabin door every morning. Called "Today's Programme" or "Cruise Compass" or "Topics," this is your basic bible of what's doing when. Do read it, even if only to know what is taking a lower priority to your desire to lie in the sun daydreaming.

Flotta Lauro has gone that idea one better and for some of its Mediterranean cruises actually put all the schedules and background information together into a bound 150-page book. The essentials you need to know to get around the ship, data on the various ports of call—including full-page photographs and city maps—and activities planned for the whole journey are all included. It takes some of the surprise out of getting up in the morning and discovering what special something has been laid on for that day, but it is an approach that lets you plan ahead.

A huge amount of other information is available to passengers. On the mammoth *Queen Elizabeth II*, there are numbers to dial on the ship's internal telephone system to get the weather forecast or the time of day; there are even different numbers to call for different languages.

Many ships operate their own internal radio system as well, with as many as six different stations (called "channels") which can be heard on receivers in each cabin. On the *Sun Viking*, there are three programs offered during most of the day: one station devoted entirely to classical music, one to the current 100 best-selling pop records (with a two-hour interlude in the music every morning and evening for news relayed from the British Broadcasting Company, Armed Forces Network, or Voice of America), and one to the same bland background music piped into the hallways and public rooms. But the "Muzak channel" also carries a lot of the programs put on by the cruise staff, so you can, for instance, hear a lecture on customs procedures or shopping at the next port from the comfort of your own room.

In addition, Royal Caribbean Line has produced a documentary film about its ships that is shown periodically through their voyages. Apart from the rather surprising sensation of sitting someplace seeing a movie of the place where you are sitting, it offers all sorts of insights into the workings of the liners and the pleasures available that you could miss just operating on your own.

On every ship, there is a big chart of the oceans through which you are sailing posted on the Promenade deck or some other central spot. You can check each day to see just how much progress you have made. And there is usually a betting pool available, where the passenger that comes closest to guessing the exact number of nautical miles traveled each day collects the entire pot.

But perhaps the most important source of information is the ship personnel themselves. The cruise director will probably offer an introductory lecture shortly after embarkation, where you can meet all the members of his staff. But at any time, they—or most any of the stewards or stewardesses—will be able to advise you what's coming up that is your precise cup of tea. The cruise staff will also arrange something special, such as a seagoing meeting of your service club, if you just request it. Again we remind you, it's all there for the asking.

14 Gastronomy Galore

With all there is to do, and with all the opportunity you have to pick and choose the activities that delight you most, there's one entertainment that all passengers share and that ranks at or near the top of everyone's list: eating. Humorist Erma Bombeck isn't really joking when she says, "The truth is, most cruises are floating cookies. Like Pavlov's dog, you are conditioned to a series of chimes. Every time the chimes ring, you loosen your belt, unzip your slacks if the zipper is concealed under an overblouse, and announce, 'Let's go eat. They're playing our song.' "

Mealtime is gala. It is the one time that all the passengers are together, and the dining room will probably be not only the largest room on the ship, but also one of the most elegant. Silver, crystal, and linen glow; some lines even run special candlelight dinners to enhance the aura of romance which is already there. Others pride themselves on always having fresh flowers on the tables.

Second sitting, because there will not be any children in the dining room, may turn out to be somewhat more dressy than first. But whichever you have chosen will be a time to bring out the long dresses for the women. (The exceptions: departure day, packing-up day just before the journey is over, and days that have been spent visiting a port.) There will be more women in long skirts than men in tuxedos or dinner jackets, but the black-tie approach is very much indicated to those who enjoy the extra fillip that formal wear adds to any occasion.

As we have said, cruising is an attempt to wed today's easy casualness with the elegance of a dressier era; at dinnertime, the elegance usually dominates. The ambience is friendly, not one of hauteur, more like a tony country club than a snooty French restaurant: The rank upon rank of service persons are there to serve you, not size you up. But since they are probably in white tie and tails, you rather feel like putting on the dog too.

The second night at sea and the night before the final one of the voyage are traditionally the nights for the most elegant dinners of all, the captain's welcome to the passengers, and the farewell. It's then that the always lavish menus sport an even grander tone: Caviar, for instance, usually shows up among the appetizers, and truffles in the sauce for the chicken. Lobster will be one of the choices for the fish course.

It is common for ships to offer six meals a day, and if dawn breakfasts on deck and 2:00 A.M. pizza parties are added to that, the total goes even higher. Every bit of that eating is included in your ticket price, so your pocketbook doesn't have to fight with your stomach. An aunt of ours used to talk about a really carefree night on the town as one in which she "wasn't looking at the right-hand side" of a menu. On a ship it's even better: There are no prices to avoid looking at.

And your stewards and waiters will be encouraging you to sample to your heart's content: The South American dinner usually offered one night on Royal Caribbean Lines, for instance, features a Venezuelan lamb ragout with coriander seasoning that is tempting to try, but which you might not want to commit yourself to as your main course. No problem. Just order it as well as a more conventional dish—roast beef, for example, is on the same menu. The sky's the limit.

The dinner menu will almost surely have more than a dozen choices of appetizer, and that provides the perfect chance to nibble at a new deli-

cacy. Mango soup, nut soup, beef tongue in green sauce, pissaladière (a French version of pizza), clams in brandy sauce, papaya juice, lingonberry juice, gougère de gruyère (a cheese cream puff), and reindeer meatballs with smoked oysters all show up in our collection of menus from recent cruises.

The lines all offer a variety of foreign dishes, as well as steaks and roast beef for passengers with less venturesome tastes. But they particularly excel in showing off native cooking: One reason some smaller countries keep fleets of liners going, after all, is a show of national pride. So the stroganoff on a Russian ship is sure to be memorable, the coq au vin on a French ship a totally different dish from the chicken stewed in cheap red wine so often passed off under that name, and, on a Norwegian ship, the chance to eat duckling stuffed with a prune and apple concoction (ande stek med svisker og epler) is one not to be missed. The Italians will regale you not only with marvelous veal main dishes, but more variety of pasta shapes and sauces than you probably realized existed. Such Costa Line ships as the Federico C, World Renaissance, Eugenio C, and Carlo C, as well as Italian Cruise Line International's newly refurbished Marconi and Galilei carry pasta chefs who do nothing but prepare the various farinaceous courses.

Remember that the cooking is being done in quantity. Honestly, in most ship kitchens, it does not measure up to the highest levels of the world's best restaurants, where each dish is prepared to order. But if the sauce is not such a perfect blending of herbs that you think it should become the standard by which all others are judged, the general quality never dips below very good. Not one of the meals aboard may be the best of your lifetime, but the level of pleasure you get in a ship's dining room over a week is apt to be above any seven days of eating out ashore. And the repertoire is so extensive that the executive chef of one liner brags that even on a month-long cruise, he never repeats a menu.

Dinners are affairs of many courses: After hors d'oeuvres and soup, at least the Italian lines will offer a pasta course; then there's a choice of fish and seafood, followed by the main course. Potatoes and a variety of vegetables—regardless of what you order, you will probably be presented with an array of at least four—and a number of salads among which to choose. A cheese course is there before dessert, if you wish, and then a selection of pastries, ice creams, and fruits. On the most gala occasions,

JUICES
Orange, grapefruit, tomato, prune, lemon.

FRUIT
Sliced orange, apple, banana, melon, fruit salad.

COMPOTES
Pear, peaches, pineapple, apricot, stewed prunes.

CEREALS
Oatmeal, Cream of Wheat, Corn Flakes, Shredded Wheat, Puffed Rice, Rice Crispies, All-bran, Farina, Semolina.

FISH
Kippered Herring, Fried fish with lemon - parsley sauce.

EGGS
Boiled, poached, scrambled, turned over, shirred with tomato.
Omelets :
Ham, mushroom, parsley, tomato, cheese, sausage, marmalade, plain, Spanish.

MEATS
Sliced bacon, country sausages, ham, pork chops, breakfast steak.

JAMS, MARMALADES AND HONEY
Orange, peach, apricot, strawberry, Greek honey.

BREADS
Toast, buns, rolls, muffins, crescents, Pancakes with syrup, honey cake, French toast.

CHEESE
Selection of cheeses - Yoghurt.

BEVERAGES
Coffee, milk, cocoa, Nescafé, Ovomaltine, Ceylon tea, Camomile, iced coffee, iced tea.

m.s. Aquarius

some ships will serve sherbets between the courses, as a way of relaxing your taste buds for the next delicacy. And on some ships, wine is included with all dinners at no extra cost.

Often the evening meal is built around a particular theme. Italian and French nights are common. More unusual is "A Night at a Medieval Castle" offered by the *Carla C;* one of the choices is a glazed leg of pork with baked apples. The *Fairsea* sometimes schedules a Pacific Dinner, where the foods range from enchiladas to coconut cream soup.

Lunches let you pick either hot or cold dishes; on sunny days at sea, there will probably be a poolside buffet set up as an alternative to the dining room lunch for those who don't want to crawl out of swimsuits. Some ships put up charcoal grills on deck and feature cooked-to-order hamburgers. The *Veendam* even offers a choice of three lunch spots: poolside, out of the sun in an informal air-conditioned lounge on Promenade deck, or the elegance of the dining room. Make a different decision each day.

Even breakfast is sumptuous: The *Emerald Seas,* for instance, lists on its menu not only twelve egg choices but also pancakes, kippered herring, finnan haddie, grits, potatoes, ham, sausage, bacon, corned beef hash, and a variety of breads, fruits, and juices. It is typical. And midmorning bouillon breaks, afternoon tea, and a lavish midnight buffet are also standard shipboard meals.

In addition, as we've indicated, a room steward who is treated right will almost surely be able to produce a tray with a sandwich, fruit, or similar sustenance should hunger strike at other moments. The Royal Viking Line stewardesses bring a fresh fruit basket for each cabin each day even without prompting.

Those are just the standard offerings. But most lines happily accommodate individual diet needs. "We have a menu for everyone," boasts Mario Anselmi, maître d' on the *Fairwind.* Whether for religious or health reasons, if you need special cooking—such as salt-free dishes—just tell your travel agent when you book your passage, and the chef will accommodate you. Be sure to remind the dining room captain when you book your table. There's no extra charge for this extra service, although a small minority of lines—Royal Caribbean is one—will not individualize their cooking.

Special treats, of course, do not have to be limited to those on special diets. If there's a main dish or dessert you particularly like, discuss it with the captain and he will probably be able to arrange for the chef to prepare it just for your table. On the big *Queen Elizabeth II,* the kitchen often fills 300 such special orders on a single day. It can handle the job because it is so huge: ovens big enough to bake 400 rolls at once, a rotisserie that can turn 200 chickens at the same time. Certainly if someone in your group is having a birthday or anniversary during the cruise, the kitchen crew will want to serve a specially decorated cake on the right day. "If you're young and pretty and it isn't your birthday, they will bake you a cake anyway," *Travel and Leisure* writer David Butwin found on the *Queen.*

Anselmi insists that one passenger who complained that his steak was too thin was suffering needlessly: "We'll make it just as thick as he wants it," the maître d' says. "Just let him tell his dining room steward. Quantity surely is no problem." It isn't: On shipboard requests for double portions are met without a batted eyelash.

All it takes is the asking. Stocks are ample. Before the *Volendam* leaves New York on a seven-day cruise to Bermuda, for instance, there are loaded aboard 37,000 pounds of meat—29,000 pounds of it beef—15,000 pounds of poultry, and 16,900 pounds of fish. Among the fresh vegetables are 4,000 pounds of celery, 2,500 pounds of onions, 2,400 pounds of tomatoes, and 1,200 pounds of cucumbers; those go with 3,600 heads of lettuce. Artichokes are a luxury: There are only 500 along for the week. But there's no stinting at all on the eggs; the normal order for the cruise is 3,000 dozen.

The *Doric* carries 400 gallons of fresh milk, 15,000 pounds of flour, 4,000 pounds of sugar, 2,000 pounds of coffee. On a recent round-the-world sailing, the *Queen* took along 35,000 bottles of wine, 33,750 pounds of lobster, and an incredible two tons of caviar. All the food is kept secure, but the caviar is behind two separate sets of locks.

One reason the *Queen* can maintain high-quality stocks, says executive chef John Bainbridge, is that "we have the best of three markets for our supplies—New York for meats and fresh vegetables; Cherbourg for French wines, snails, and other specialties; and Southampton for caviar shipped from Russia, for partridge, grouse, and pheasant."

Eating is a central activity on a cruise for more reasons than the fact that there's so much food from which to choose. For one thing, the salty sea air really stimulates appetites, so passengers come to the table with a

ms. Carla C.   CURACAO
                                Monday - 1978

Luncheon

JUICES
Grapefruit   Tomato   Prune   Pineapple   Apple

HORS D'OEUVRE
"Pancetta,,   Mortadella   Griek Salad
Green and Red Peppers   Fish Mayonnaise   Mackerel in Olive Oil
Egg-Plants Vinaigrette   Celery Salad Oriental

SOUPS
Hot and Cold Beef Broth   "Stracciatella alla Romana,,
                    Manhattan Chowder

FARINACEOUS
"Manicotti alla Amalfitana,,   "Linguine with Meat Sauce,,

EGGS
Poached, Belle Hélène   Scrambled, Balzac
       Shirred, Monegasque   American Omelette

FISH
Grouper Fillets, Capers in Buttered Sauce

For Special Orders and Diets Please consult the Maître d'Hôte

ENTREES
Escalope of Veal a la Florentina with Buttered Spinacks
Fresh Fruit Salad, Cottage Cheese or Sour Cream

Continental Speciality
Savoury Hungarian Goulash with Parslied Potatoes
Cubes of cross ribs of beef, browned in oil, cooked with chopped onions, tomatoes, celery,
paprika and savory cream

FROM THE GRILL (15 minutes)
Minute Steak of Prime Ribs - French Fried Potatoes
Broiled Spring Chicken "Diavola., with Bacon

COLD DISHES

Pâté de Foie Gras, Maison	Stuffed Breast of Veal, Mixed Salad
Corred Beef Brisket, Horseradish Sauce	Roast Chicken, Chow-Chow
Assorted Cold Cuts New Jersey Ham	Roast Beef English Style

VEGETABLES
Brussels Sprouts   Turnips Provençale

POTATOES
French Fried   Steamed   Parslied

SALADS
Iceberg   Mixed   Beetroots

DRESSINGS
Roquefort   Russian   Lemon and Oil   Remoulade

CHEESES
Emmenthal   Mozzarella   Gouda   Gorgonzola

ICE CREAM
Strawberry   Vanilla   Chocolate   Rum   Peach

DESSERTS
Nougat Tart   Lemon Jell-O   Italian Pastry

CANNED FRUIT
Pears   Pineapples   Apricots   Cherries   Peaches

STEWED FRUIT
Baked Apples   Prunes   Baked Pears

FRESH FRUIT
Basket of Fresh Fruit in Season

BEVERAGES
Coffee   Demitasse   Tea   Sanka   Hag   Cocoa   Boldo   Camomile   Milk

special zest that makes even standard fare seem extra fine. "That's the best Rice Krispies I ever had in my life," New Orleans newspaperwoman Mabel C. Simmons heard another passenger on the *Odessa* say after the first breakfast.

But there's more to it: Not only is the food abundant and tastily prepared, but the service has a style and attentiveness that have all but disappeared from most eateries. "You dine better and more elegantly on almost any of today's sleek cruise ships than in most restaurants on land," says James Villas, who often writes about the good life. He lauds such touches on the QE2 as wrapping lemon wedges in cheesecloth so there's no danger of seeds getting onto your food, and serving dinnertime martinis in an iced carafe, with a frosted glass at its side. The midnight buffets are feasts for the eyes as well as the stomach, with the food elegantly decorated and arranged. The managers of Royal Caribbean Lines not long ago figured that twenty-eight persons work on putting together the showiest buffet on a cruise, each putting in an average of more than ten hours on the job.

The waiters will urge you to try new dishes, will explain what's in mysterious sauces, will advise which choice is going to make you most happy. With every item available to every passenger, there's none of the incentive to push certain dishes that are moving slowly or to goad a customer into making a more expensive selection.

Most waiters take a positively paternalistic pleasure in seeing you stuff yourself, and they encourage you to start at the top of the menu and have one (or preferably two) of each item on the way down. There is much good-natured joshing among the stewards about whose tables have the best eaters. Ladies who are reluctant to give up their calorie counting are the object of special persuasion, especially on ships with Mediterranean crews who do not subscribe to the idea that "you can never be too thin." It may seem cloying on land, and you wouldn't tolerate it from the headwaiter at Delmonico's; it's all part of the pampering wrap-you-in-cotton-batting approach.

There's another aspect to memorable dining besides the food and ambience and service: your companions. We have already discussed the pluses and minuses you should weigh in your initial request for a table assignment. But remember: You are not stuck with your first placement. Just as a couple may want midjourney to ask for a switch to a bigger table with new-made friends, those who have opted for a table with company can ask for a reassignment if the company turns out to be a drag.

As Jane O'Reilly, who often writes for *House & Garden,* says, "Do not spend a second worrying about the boring people you have left abandoned, the maître d'hotel will find them some nice new friends—he knows people better than anyone else on the ship." And the table-switching game isn't just a one-time thing. If you find the second assignment no more simpatico, hie yourself back to the maître d' for another try. (The more he does for you, of course, the bigger should be the tip you give him at journey's end. And if you ask for a new table more than once, it would be a good idea to slip him the little extra amount right then.)

It hardly seems necessary to say it, but finding the right mealtime companions is even more important for single travelers than for those who already have along at least one person whose company they enjoy.

When you bump into your former tablemates on deck or at the ship's movie, there's no need for either apology or explanation. But if you feel pressured to offer some reason for the change, any casual white lie will do: You had struck up a friendship with your new companions and they just insisted that you join them for meals, or the maître d' had asked you to change because he so wanted your replacements to meet the people you left behind, or even, "Frankly, my dear, although I am embarrassed to mention it, that marvelous perfume of yours seems to have brought on an awful allergic reaction in me." That should guarantee that you'll have to have no more than a nodding acquaintance with them the rest of the voyage, and dumps all the blame in their lap.

With all these incentives to eat it up, it is probably unrealistic to expect to come back from a cruise the same weight you left. Even a conscientious regimen of morning runs around the deck isn't going to use up all the extra calories. Mary McFadden, a rail-thin type, says that on her annual summer cruise, she tries to hold herself to three courses at dinner, plus "a small dessert." On a recent voyage to Alaska, she remembers, "I always ordered whatever the fresh fish was: salmon, halibut, Dungeness crab, crawfish, swordfish, cutthroat trout—very slimming to eat all that fish. You can have it broiled, fried, breaded, baked, steamed, marinated, sometimes served hot, sometimes cold."

Some ships do have special selections on their menus for dieters. The *Rotterdam,* for instance, offers calorie counters a special salad each

CARIBBEAN CRUISES

Gala Farewell Dinner

Soavity Dream Cocktail
Fresh Malossol Caviar, American Dressing
Strasbourg Goose Liver, Meat Jelly
Smoked Nova Scotia Salmon, Garlic Bread
Jumbo Shrimps, Brandied Sauce
Sweet Prosciutto, Spiced Cantalupo Melon

Hot: Crab Meat Au Gratin in Coquille

Original Bird's Nest Consommé, Golden Straw
Chicken Tortellini Soup   Peas Cream St.Germain

Chilled: Velvet of Palm Heart

Grilled Sole Fillets, Lemon Butter
Casserole of Lobster a la Mode du Chef

Rock Cornish Game Hen "Oceanic"
Plume Veal Rosettes with White Mushrooms

Mandarine Sherbet

Broiled Fillet Mignon, Bernaise Sauce
Roast Rack of Lamb Printanier, Natural Gravy

Asparagus Salad   Garden Vegetables

Flaming Baked Alaska Valentino
Moka Spumone   Paradise Cake
Sugar Basket with Original Friandises

Champagne

Vodka   *Espresso*

Thursday, February 23, 1978

lunchtime: a combination of Alaska salmon, cottage cheese, and tropical fruits one day; or strips of ham, turkey, ox tongue, Swiss cheese, and apple another. Its featured Rotterdam Salad has a yogurt dressing over orange sections, watermelon cubes, julienne of chicken, and thin sliced peppers on shredded lettuce.

But we think that saying no too often to the opulent offerings spoils a lot of the fun of a cruise. Better to follow the course of Ana Johnson, a family relations officer for the Connecticut Court of Common Pleas, on a recent cruise to South America: She dieted *before* the vacation, so the extra pounds acquired on shipboard would just put her back to her normal weight.

Some cruise directors make passengers' interest in food into an activity. A tour of the kitchen is available on almost every ship, and you should take it. But some go beyond that into actual cooking demonstrations. The soup chef on the *Odessa,* for instance, explains how to make borscht—there are 100 different kinds, and not all are based on beets—and the proper way to eat it. That is with wooden spoons, and each passenger walks away from the show with his or her own spoon as a souvenir.

On Holland America ships, the chefs teach everyone who's interested how to make—what else—cheese fondue. Here's the recipe they use:

> Pour two cups of dry white wine into a fondue dish and add a peeled clove of garlic. Bring the wine to a boil for almost two minutes, then remove the garlic and lower the heat so the wine is barely simmering. Stirring all the time, add handfuls of a mixture of coarsely grated Dutch Gouda cheese and some cornstarch (a scant teaspoon of cornstarch for each cup of cheese). Make sure each handful is well melted before adding the next, and when the entire mixture is creamy smooth, add two tablespoons of Kirsch liqueur and a little salt, black pepper, and nutmeg (on the ship, it's freshly grated). The fondue dish is then put over an alcohol burner regulated to just keep it lightly bubbling, and the passengers get to swirl cubes of French bread in the yummy mixture.

Vacationers who repeat the recipe at home are assured not only of a successful party, but of a flood of happy memories, a little reliving of the pleasure of the cruise. That's why other lines, too, encourage customers to take home with them recipes from some of the showpiece dishes they enjoyed on board. Here, for example, is a home version of Lobster Virgin Island as served on the *Doric:*

Melt in a pan 2 oz. of unsalted butter, then add four oz. of olive oil. Put into the pan two lobsters, opened vertically, with tails cut and claws crushed. Add two small glasses of cognac and one glass of dry white wine, 2 pounds of peeled and mashed tomatoes, 1 tablespoon of chopped leek, 1 garlic clove, a small bunch of tarragon, and half a laurel leaf. Cover and cook for 35 minutes, adding small amounts of water if necessary. Then remove the lobster meat from the shell, and keep it warm.

Strain the rest of the sauce, and put it back on to cook, adding another small glass of cognac, another teaspoon of tarragon (finely chopped this time), a dash of cayenne pepper, and four ounces of heavy cream. Be careful not to let the mixture boil.

In another pan, cook in butter and garlic a pound of mushrooms, sliced very thin. Then add them to the sauce, pour over the lobster, and serve with rice.

If you'd prefer a meat main dish, this is how they make Medaillon of Veal Orloff on Royal Caribbean ships:

Oil a boneless 3½ lb. loin of veal and sprinkle with salt and pepper. Roast the veal at 400°F for 45 minutes and then continue roasting at 325° for one hour, basting with pan juices. While meat is roasting, make Mornay sauce and mushrooms duxelle as follows:

Melt 2 oz. butter and stir in 2 oz. flour, then add 1 pt. boiling milk, stirring until sauce is smooth. Mix 2 egg yolks with 2½ oz. light cream and gradually add to sauce, stirring constantly. Then stir in 1 tsp. salt, ⅛ tsp. white pepper, three tbsp. grated Parmesan cheese, and 1 oz. butter cut in small pieces. Set aside.

For mushrooms duxelle, melt 1 oz. butter or margarine and lightly sauté 3 tbsp. finely chopped onions. Then, in the same pan, sauté 4 oz. finely chopped mushrooms. Stir until all moisture is evaporated. Slice meat into medaillons, top each with mushrooms duxelle and Mornay sauce. Run under broiler to glaze. Serve the glazed medaillons with natural gravy from veal roast.

As we've indicated, pasta courses are standard on many ships' bills of fare. Although Princess Line is now part of the big British P&O shipping empire, the service crew is still Italian, including chef Paolo Bonanno, who offers passengers this variation on a standard lasagna:

First make two sauces, béchamel and bolognese.

Béchamel is made by blending 2 tablespoons of flour, a pinch of salt, and a pinch of freshly-ground pepper into 2 tablespoons of melted butter. Heat 2 cups of light cream with a slice of onion, and then add the cream gradually to the butter-flour mixture. Stir until it thickens, and then boil for 2 minutes.

The bolognese sauce starts by melting butter in a frying pan, adding oil, and frying together all the following ingredients: 1 pound of coarsely ground meat (beef, pork, and veal, mixed in the proportion that most pleases you), 1 chopped onion, 3 minced garlic cloves, 2 chopped carrots, 2 stalks chopped celery, 1 sprig chopped parsley, ¼ teaspoon ground bay leaf, ¼ teaspoon ground rosemary, ½ cup beef broth, and 2 pounds of tomato sauce. Fry the mixture until the meat is brown, then add ½ pound sliced mushrooms and cook for 1 minute more. Put in ½ cup dry white wine, and let the wine cook off. Then put in 3 tablespoons of tomato paste and cook until the sauce is thick—approximately 90 minutes.

Bonanno makes his own lasagna noodles of flour, eggs, and oil, but you can use ready-made strips, cooked in salted water. Assemble the lasagna by putting on the bottom of a deep baking dish a layer of the thick bolognese sauce, then a layer of béchamel, then the pasta strips, then slices of Fontina cheese, and keep repeating the layering process until all the ingredients are used up. Bake in a 350° oven until the top is lightly browned.

Dessert is one of the courses in which the ship menu planners like to show off the traditions of their native lands. There will be French pastries on Paquet liners and baklava and halva on the *Castalia* and this trifle, the most British of desserts, on the *QE2*:

Put a round of yellow sponge cake in the bottom of a large bowl, and sprinkle with sherry. Top it with raspberries and slivered almonds, repeating layers of cake and the fruit-nut mix until the bowl is filled. Then pour custard over the top, generously enough so it will seep down around the sides and moisten the layers below.

Refrigerate the desert until you are ready to serve it, but be sure to allow enough time for it to jell. Just before serving, top it with whipped cream, and decorate with cherries.

To complement the good dishes, there really should be fine wine, of course, and such imbibables are very much part of a vacation at sea. *Esquire*'s Stephen Birnbaum says, "For the two-fisted drinker, a cruise trip is almost a license to steal, since liquor and wine prices on board are generally quite a bit less than those at home or onshore." Even those more moderate in their drinking habits can appreciate the bargains.

The main reason for the low prices is that ships in international waters have to pay no nation's taxes on the liquor they use. In mid-1978, it was common for a shipboard Scotch to cost less than a dollar. With inflation constantly pushing up prices, that specific figure may be out of date by the time you read this, but it is safe to say that a mixed drink on board ship should cost you no more than half what it would in the cocktail lounge of a big hotel in any large U.S. city. Carnival Cruise Lines, for instance, offers a real French champagne for less than $7.50 a bottle.

And there's something very soothing about sipping a long and frothy drink as you glide through the blue waters. The kind of rum concoctions that seem too sweet or too frivolous back home—a piña colada or a banana daiquiri—are just right when delivered midafternoon to your deck chair by an ever-ready steward.

Part of the fun of drinking on a cruise is trying such new things. Some ships even develop their own specialties. The Oceanic, which as far as we know is available only on that ship, is made with an ounce and a half each of rum and pineapple juice, a quarter ounce of grapefruit juice, an eighth of an ounce each of dry vermouth and grenadine, and just a dash of Galliano. The bartender garnishes it with a slice of orange and a maraschino cherry and it goes down awfully easily.

The QE2 features a different specialty cocktail every day. One is the Afrikanda, made of South African brandy and a special South African liqueur called Van Der Hum, flavored with tangerines and herbs; orange juice and soda are added to the more potent ingredients. On the Sun Viking, the bartender on duty after dinner in the Merry Widow Lounge even offers ladies a Chameleon cocktail, mixed to order of liqueurs and cordials blended to duplicate the exact color of their dresses.

Wines with dinner are part of the ambience, and ships keep a varied cellar to select from. The QE2 stocks 2,000 bottles of champagne for a

five-day voyage. Again, the prices are far lower than the norm for land-based fine restaurants. There will be a sommelier in the dining room—on most ships you can identify him at once by the chain around his neck with a small silver cup dangling from it—who will be most helpful about picking from his stock. And he won't try to foist off the most expensive bottle on you. Many menus contain a suggested wine to complement the featured entrée, and it is almost always a wise pick of moderate price. And champagne or its local equivalent, such as Asti Spumante on an Italian ship, goes with everything and strikes just the festive note you want on a cruise.

(Drinks are one of the few exceptions to the one-price-covers-everything rule. You *do* pay for your own, except for table wines on some lines. If you've had wine at table on ships that do not provide it, the sommelier will bring your bill at the end of the cruise.)

There will be cocktail parties among the activities. The captain will host a big party for all passengers. Other get-togethers are put on by the ship's officers for, sometimes, those who have sailed previously on that line, or for passengers traveling alone. These are almost always on the first days of the voyage, to help passengers strike up friendships.

But in addition, you'll be invited to smaller gatherings given by passengers in their own cabins to get to know better friends they've made at the next table at dinner or the next deck chair. If you want to provide such a do, just talk it over with your cabin steward. He'll arrange drinks and hors d'oeuvres without a hitch.

15 Special Needs and Special Interests

The reason ships are so heavily staffed is so there will always be someone knowledgeable available to answer any question from any passenger. Problems should be nonexistent. But because some travelers have special needs or special interests and want to know details ahead of time, we'll try to fill them in right now.

Young Voyagers

Cruise ships offer particular joys to those traveling with children. There's simply no land-based equivalent that gives kids so many different things to do while presenting parents such a low worry quotient. You can give them the run of the ship, confident that they will not wander too far or have trouble finding their way back to your cabin or designated rendezvous spot.

A ship as a small self-contained world is an easy universe for a child to grasp. We've found with our own daughters, when they were as young as seven, that they immediately understood which deck was where and how to get from one public room to another; they were constantly giving directions to befuddled elders. We would, of course, like to think that they are especially bright and seawise, but the fact is that the same sort of stories are told by so many parents—and so many ship passengers who have been shown the way to their destinations by preteens—that we have to believe it is a general ability that children have.

It makes sense, really: The very definable limits of the liner's world make it something even small children can understand; there are none of those vague anxieties about what lies beyond the periphery that make new places worrisome for some children.

And there is reason for children to search out every nook on a ship, for so many of them hold activities for the youngsters. All big ships have special children's playrooms for the youngest ones, filled with toys and games, where there is scheduled entertainment geared to young audiences: puppet shows, cartoon movies, masquerade parties. On the *Mardi Gras* this room is decorated with a delightful mural of friendly jungle animals, the giraffe munching leaves off a palm tree and the lion peering hesitantly out from the bushes. The furniture is plastic, light but durable, in bright primary colors.

The ships have a crew charged entirely with keeping children happy. On the *Fairwind,* for instance, there are five members assigned to children's activities. The children are generally kept so well entertained that a passenger on one Caribbean cruise on the QE2 says she wasn't aware of any children on the ship until she suddenly happened on a party with 160 of them!

When children reach the point where they want more independence than the bambini room allows them, which tends to be around third-grade level, they'll hunt out other entertainments. The pool, of course, is a popular spot; some ships have game rooms with pinball machines and slot machines that seem like magnets for children; although technically most ships declare the gambling devices off limits to minors, that is not the most enforced rule aboard. The cruise director and his staff will probably plan special events so that teens on board can meet each other. The *Achille Lauro,* for instance, has a discotheque party for "the young people" at 5:00 P.M. on the second day after departure. During the summer, when kids are out of school, the *Rotterdam* sets aside a special room, designated The Place, with both pinball machines and a jukebox, designed as a teen hangout. But we've noticed the adolescents seem to find each other even without such official aids.

Lorna Caine, an administrative coordinator at Condé Nast Publications, went on a cruise to Bermuda with her husband and two daughters when the girls were five and two and a half. She gave them their suppers, ordered a day in advance, in their room each evening, then tucked them into bed. "Then we had time to change for our late dinner sitting," she says, "and at eight-thirty our nice steward would arrive to baby-sit and the evening was ours."

But most families, at least when the children are a bit older, eat dinner together in the dining room. And on a two-sitting ship, that means it has to be the first sitting. But at other times the children may like to be with their siblings or newfound friends. They frequently prefer the informal lunches at poolside to those in the dining room—especially if they are featuring charcoal-grilled hamburgers—and almost always the movies and evening variety entertainment are suitable for audiences of all ages.

With children as with adults, a ship is the one vacation that lets you do whatever you like. The family that sees a holiday as a time to stick together and spend more time with each other than the busy workaday weeks allow can run the gamut from morning to night, with hot bouts of shuffleboard and hours-long games of Monopoly and the desultory conversation that goes with basking in a deck chair. The family that likes to

pursue individual adventures, then exchange anecdotes over dinner, can let each member follow his or her individual bent, sure of both safety and satisfaction. You write your own ticket.

But when help is needed, especially with very young children, it is there. Of course, there are high chairs and booster seats available in the dining room, and infant foods will be prepared if you simply have your travel agent let the line know you will be traveling with a toddler. Baby-sitters are available to allow parents to revel beyond their youngsters' bedtimes, but most often are not really necessary: Your steward or stewardess is never out of sight of the cabin door, and simply telling the attendant that a young passenger is abed will ensure a frequent peek in and constant watchfulness. Some ships even have an intercom system that can be switched on to let the steward hear any whines coming from a child-occupied cabin, although our daughters look on that device as just a bit too intrusive to be tolerated.

Handicapped Persons

In the past decade, a lot of individual and governmental attention has been given to the special traveling problems of persons in wheelchairs, or who use walkers, or who are otherwise handicapped. But while there are books and reports and pamphlets about bus, plane, and train accommodations for the handicapped, very little has been written about the special virtues of a cruise for a vacationer with less-than-normal mobility. And that's a shame, because a cruise can be a great vacation for a handicapped person.

Even to the traveler confined to a wheelchair, literally all of the ship is easily available. Many banks of elevators connect all the decks. And for persons who walk with difficulty, it is comforting to know that all the hallways are equipped with easy-to-grip handrails. In the individual cabins, there are handrails in such spots as the bathrooms.

As we have pointed out, service persons abound. Both cabins and bathrooms have call buttons to summon help in an emergency, and a doctor is always on call: no worry about waiting while he drives in from the nearest village.

Boarding and disembarkation procedures minimize the problem of a handicapped traveler having to cope with his or her own baggage, and most lines will make readily available a wheelchair for passengers who generally do not need one but find it important traveling the long distances from check-in points to the ship itself. Just tell your travel agent to make the request when you book your cruise.

The ship's medical department will have wheelchairs on hand, but passengers who need them for the entire journey are expected to bring their own. They should be the collapsible sort, no more than twenty-four inches wide. The QE2 and many other ships have staterooms especially designed for those confined to a wheelchair, with especially wide doorways, and ramps over the curb that is in front of most ship cabin doors. The lines work with travel agents to see that handicapped vacationers get these accommodations, but they should be booked earlier than most other cabins.

The big plus for handicapped travelers on a cruise, however, is not that facilities are designed so they can get around, but that the whole approach to travel is congruent with their needs. There are spacious public rooms: One never need be in a crowd. Air conditioning throughout most ships guarantees that the temperature will be comfortable. The motion is constant, without the jerky acceleration and deceleration that are especially bothersome to the handicapped.

"One of the general characteristics of being handicapped is a slowing-down of many physical actions, including walking, which creates considerable inconvenience in a time-pressured travel environment," a study on travel barriers for the handicapped done by Abt Associates found. But a cruise is the very opposite of a "time-pressured travel environment"— you are free to do what you want when you want, and if getting to dinner takes you a bit longer, you can simply start a bit earlier for the dining room. It's hard to imagine taking care of all the needs of hundreds of vacations with less regimentation.

The same Abt report, written for the Office of Economic and Systems Analysis of the U.S. Department of Transportation, concluded that "unpredictable changes in procedure create disproportionate trouble for the disabled traveler." An airplane bound for London that is diverted to Amsterdam is a headache for everyone on board, but can present greater problems for travelers with physical infirmities. It seldom happens that a cruise ship must deviate from its planned itinerary. But, more important, when it does happen, the potential for trouble is minimal. A traveler may be disappointed if a storm prevents docking at an island he particularly wanted to visit, but bed for the night, ample food, and medical attention are with him. The ship really is your home, and even if it changes course, you're still at home.

Camera Bugs

Everyone should capture some of the fun of a cruise on film. If you're a photographer of the Instamatic sort (we used to call that the Brownie sort), simply snap away much as you would inside your own home. Film is stocked at the health- and beauty-aids store aboard your ship, at least in the most common sizes and speeds, but the shops have been known to run out during a voyage. You can hunt for it at ports of call, of course, but that wastes precious time and it is apt to be more expensive than at the discount store back home. So it's wisest to play it safe and bring along all the film and flashcubes you think you're likely to need.

Keep your camera in a case at all times when you are not actually shooting—a plastic storage bag will do the job quite nicely. You want to protect against the corrosive potential of the salty air. Salt spray can be especially damaging, and it is a distinct possibility if you have your camera along on a tender going from ship to shore at one of the ports of call. If the camera is splashed, wipe it off with a towel dipped in *fresh* water as soon as possible. Then pray. Have a camera shop look at it when you get back home, but in the interim the ship photographer may be able to tell you if any serious damage has been done.

All ships have photographers aboard who take and sell pictures in the dining room, at the masquerade party, and on similar set occasions. But it's best to supplement them with your own shots. Apart from your personal moments that are worthy of photographing, the ship encourages photographers by setting aside special sessions for them to have exclusive access to certain sights. One night, for instance, picture takers will probably be let in early to the grand midnight buffet to capture its carved ice centerpieces, decorated hams, and pyramids of shrimp before waiting passengers demolish the display. For movie takers, many ships have title cards set up on port days so photographers can establish the locale with a real pro look before stepping ashore.

When you venture onto deck for pictures, the same sun intensity that makes us warn you so insistently about overexposing your skin can play havoc with the exposure of your pictures. If all you're going for is snapshots to paste into an album for the grandchildren or to send to Aunt Minnie, probably the simplest answer is to concentrate your picture taking inside the ship or, if you venture on deck, to stick to shaded areas. If you do want to snap poolside pictures in full sun, use a magazine or hat to shade your lens.

For serious photographers, that very special play of light that can cause troubles also opens a potential for uniquely dramatic pictures. It takes some advance planning, patience, and a willingness to have a few shots you don't want anyone to see. Don't trust instinct: Check your exposure meter after virtually every shot.

Begin with filters, of course. A medium-yellow filter is the standard for marine scenes; choosing an orange instead will make the water darker, heighten contrasts. If you are trying to shoot the approach to a harbor, where the glistening water is embraced by dark foliage, try a light-green filter: It will dilute some of the strong chiaroscuro effect, but give you excellent sky tones.

For color, the slightly pinkish filter known as a skylight filter (common before the days of Kodachrome II) can still be of help in the kind of glare the sun gives at sea. A polarizing filter is also useful, but only if the sun angle is right. Ideally, it should be at a ninety-degree angle to a line between you and your subject. If you are shooting straight ahead, that means directly overhead. The polarizing filter will darken sky tones, but not distort color relationships. It cuts through haze, giving you pictures of harbors that are clearer than the scene was to your naked eye. Some friends call that a plus, others prefer the atmospheric aura the polarizer eliminates.

"Backlights can be used to give a shimmering radiance, a feeling of animation to water scenes," says Helen Bruce, author of a standard handbook on photography. "By sending elongated shadows toward the camera, backlight imparts an illusion of greater depth, as well as a more pronounced separation of lights and darks; a low camera angle further increases the depth illusion." But remember that the friends you put in the foreground of such pictures will emerge as silhouettes.

You will probably want to decrease exposure a full stop from what you would normally expect. By playing with apertures and speed, you can get different effects in your ocean shots. A small opening and slow speed will help you capture the sense of that enormous expanse of moving water. But opening the lens more and moving the speed to, say, 1/250 of a second can let you take home the details of the foam droplets around the roiling waves.

Some critics feel that most shots of that seemingly limitless mass of water are inherently boring. They remind us of the mood of peace and isolation that we feel makes a cruise vacation so very special. But if you want more conventional composition, with birds or other ships as contrasting elements to the water, expect to need a telescopic lens or at least one of long focal length. Even objects that seem close when nothing but the ocean separates you will turn up as nothing more than pinpoints in shots taken with normal lenses. Obviously, your best chance to get other elements in the water comes when the ship is near a port, although passing another ship on the open seas is an event not uncommon yet always exciting.

Technology Buffs

One of the joys of ocean travel is that you can leave all the problems to someone else. Your voyage is in the hands of seasoned experts, and you can just sit back and know you're getting where you're supposed to be, with never a worry about how it all works. But for those who get their kicks out of knowing the mechanics of the surroundings, a ship can be a fascinating school.

As we've already said, the engine room is generally off limits to passengers, but a visit to the bridge—where the navigation is done and commands issued—can usually be arranged. The engine room really houses more than one power source: On the *Sun Viking*, for instance, there are four engines, each a 9-cylinder nonreversible single-action, two-stroke model built in Finland from Swiss designs. Each engine is capable of an output of 4,500 horsepower at 410 revolutions per minute. They are coupled in pairs to the propeller shafts, but can be run individually, depending on the speed the Captain wants to maintain. With all four going, the ship can hit 21 knots (24 land miles an hour), but with only one, it can cruise easily at 12 knots.

The propellers themselves are massive. On the *Sun Viking*, they measure 12 feet in diameter. And on the biggest ship of all sailing today, the *QE2*, they are each 19 feet across, weighing 31 tons each. In addition to the aft propellers, some ships have a supplemental steering aid forward, called a bow thruster and mounted in the middle of a tunnel at the very tip, giving the captain such precise control that he can dock the ship in some harbors without using tugs.

Other machinery is devoted not to moving the ship through the water, but to providing for those on board: the electrical system, for example. Ships carry their own water conversion systems to desalinize seawater so it can be used for drinking, cooking, and washing. One ship produces 60,000 gallons of fresh water a day. But those systems are supplemented by huge freshwater storage tanks—holding perhaps a quarter of a million gallons—which are refilled at some ports en route.

Ships use a variety of navigational devices, to be ready for any weather conditions. Loran, sonar, and similar electronic methods provide precise readings of the ship's location when the sky is soupy, but older methods—sighting by stars, the compass, and good old eyeballing—are still important in ship navagation. In fact, may of the rules of the sea are expressly designed to warn the sailor on traditional watch just what is where in that vast sea out there. Ships must, for instance, have mounted on the forward mast or some similar spot what is in essence a headlight: a powerful light that casts a beam visible for at least five miles over an arc of twenty compass points.

You can see much farther than that at sea, since, on a clear day, there's nothing in your sight line until the curve of the earth itself makes it drop off from view. From one of the higher decks on your ship, at 50 feet above the water level, the horizon will be 8.2 nautical miles away, or almost 9.5 land miles. From the navigation bridge, the line of sight is usually close to 10 nautical miles.

In addition to the language of lights, ships also use a language of flags. The International Flag Code standardizes shapes and colors for the letters of the alphabet and numerals, so any ship can spell out a message in flags that any other shipboard personnel can read. A white rectangle alongside a notched K-shaped section in blue is *A*, a notched all-red flag is

B, and so forth. Some of the flags have shorthand meanings: A square separated diagonally into yellow and red sections means not only *O,* but also "man overboard"; a ship hoisting *P-Y-U* (a blue square with a white square in its center, a square with red and yellow diagonal stripes, and one with red and white squares in a checkerboard pattern) is wishing a good journey to another ship.

The ship also carries flags designating its own nationality and the ensign of its owners. At sea these will fly from the mast; when approaching a port, they will be hoisted on the yardarm. When the ship is actually standing in a foreign port, custom is for the flag showing its country of registration to be moved to a flagpole at the stern of the ship. Other flags that you will see as the ship approaches port are the yellow-and-blue striped flag used for the letter *G,* which means a pilot is needed, and the red and white flag that signifies a pilot from that port is actually on board.

Ships give off signals for the ears as well as the eyes. A single short blast of the whistle, for instance, means that the ship is about to steer more to starboard (right). Two blasts mean a veering to port. When storms or fog seriously reduce visibility, ships give one long blast of the whistle every two minutes, as an additional warning of their position. But if the conditions get so bad that the ship actually stops at sea, the warning signal is increased to a pair of long blasts every two minutes.

Wind velocity is still important to sailors, even though their motive power now comes from big engines down below. Certainly the seas are choppier, and holding the ship steady a lot harder, when winds are high. To measure the wind strength, seafarers still use a scale developed in 1806 by Sir Francis Beaufort, a British admiral. It ranges from 0 to 12, and we wish you a sailing on which it never registers above 6.

If the wind is blowing at between 3 and 7 miles an hour, it will be a 1 on the Beaufort scale. A 5 means the wind is traveling between 21 and 25 miles an hour, which will be dubbed a "fresh breeze," which is somewhat stiffer than a "moderate breeze." A 6 is still nice, but a 7—winds up to 35 miles an hour—begins to be gale force. An 11 in Beaufort measure is an out-and-out storm, with winds between 61 and 70 miles an hour; worse than that and you are in a hurricane.

16 Taking Care of Yourself

All cruise ships must, by law, have a doctor aboard, and adequate facilities to handle almost any medical emergency. (That's why freighters do not carry more than twelve passengers; it is the upper limit before the physician rules go into effect.) The doctor has regular office hours for the less pressing problems—something for sniffles that keep hanging on, or dispensing an ointment for a skin allergy you picked up from exotic tropical flora—but is available twenty-four hours a day for cabin calls when necessary. You will be billed for the consultation and medication at rates that tend to run just a bit less then prevailing onshore fees in the United States, but any treatment for injuries from shipboard accidents is traditionally free. That's not likely to be more than a child's skinned knee, but there are times when rough seas can actually toss around deck chairs— and even passengers—so some more serious bumps occur.

The doctor will be assisted by a staff of nurses, and they have at their disposal a fully equipped infirmary—really a small hospital—where even emergency surgery can be performed. Chances are remote that you'll need such facilities, but it is consoling to know they are available.

There is, however, a more common shipboard health problem that is not quite a thing of the past: seasickness. Cruise Lines International Association, which has the job of luring more passengers to liners, says that seasickness is not really a problem. "Improved stabilizers on modern ships, advance availability of accurate weather information, and development of effective preventive medication have, for the most part, eliminated the incidence of motion sickness," a CLIA booklet insists.

And there's certainly a great deal of truth in the claim. The old image of lines of wobbling passengers, green of complexion, staggering to railside, is just not going to be found on an up-to-date liner, even during a rough North Atlantic crossing. And remember that most cruising is done in much calmer waters; the Caribbean and the Mediterranean are usually placid seas.

But the same gentle rolling that provides such a distinctive delight to some cruising fans may well induce a bit of wooziness in others, especially on the first day or two, until your body adjusts. When leaving from New York, there'a a spot where the waters roil a bit around Cape Hatteras, some six hours after departure. It's a good idea to take some motion-sickness medicine preventively if the idea worries you. Passengers who are tense about something are a lot more prone to the malady than those who are relaxed, which is good news, since the whole idea of cruising is to leave your troubles behind you. It is estimated that one cruise passenger in twenty suffers from seasickness: relatively low odds, but little solace if that one in twenty is you.

Dramamine or some other standard motion-sickness medication is readily available on board ship; like treatment for accidents, it is free. It is so freely dispensed, in fact, that pills are often available from your cabin steward, without a visit to the doctor. They are widely taken, quite safe formulations, but we still think it is best to check with your own doctor before a journey to make sure that he knows of no special reason that you should not take them. If he has doubts about dimenhydrinate (the chemical name for the most common active ingredient in motion-sickness medication) for you—some doctors think, for instance, that it should not be taken by patients who are at the same time taking certain antibiotics—get him to prescribe an alternative, and carry it along, just in case.

Everyone has a favorite regimen for the traveler suffering from seasickness. Research done by the U.S. military in the 1940s is pretty conclusive that you'll feel better during an attack of *mal de mer* if you keep your eyes closed. Lying on your side helps, since it keeps in balance the fluid in the semicircular canals, where imbalance contributes to a feeling of motion sickness.

Some of the self-appointed experts insist you should eat as much as you can manage, others that you should give your stomach a rest. Some advise taking Vitamin B6. Rosalind Massow, a contributing editor to *l'Officiel USA*, says that "dry food like toast or crackers will help you, but liquid will aggravate the condition." But one standard desk guide for physicians says that the victim in dire straits should drink lots of fluids, but in small doses. The answer, obviously, is that treatment is highly individual, with one passenger's salvation merely being an additional source of agony for a suffering fellow voyager. Personally, we like Jim Villas's advice best: "I've learned over the years," he says, "that nothing calms a queasy stomach any better than a split of champagne."

In any event, on a cruise you can be sure that calm waters lie ahead, and, with the stabilizers and antiroll devices, a bad day is virtually sure to be followed by a good one, when the head clears, the stomach settles, and you're ready for all the fun the ship has to offer.

That very fun can itself, of course, create health problems. We're not going to lecture here about hangovers or other morning-after prices paid for high living: There's nothing special about the effects of revelry at sea, although admittedly temptation at times seems stronger. But there is one pleasure that is particularly dangerous at sea: soaking up the sun. So watch out.

We suspect you are determined to come back from your cruise with the kind of deep tan that elicits envy from neighbors and co-workers. And we admit that lolling in a deck chair, with a steward at the ready to satisfy your slightest whim, is one of the special delights of a vacation at sea. But the sun at sea has a burning power far greater than it does on land, and you simply must be careful.

Here's a safe rule of thumb about how much to allow your unprotected skin to be exposed to the sun each day: Take ten to fifteen minutes sunning the first day, and increase your time by five minutes each day after that. Now that sun protection lotions are being labeled to let you judge their relative blocking qualities, you can extend your sunning time if you start out with partially protected skin. But to be safe, halve the time increments the labels suggest; if you are using a lotion that says it lets you stay out four times as long as you could with no protection, figure that at sea that means twice as long. And remember that as you are stretched out in a deck chair, your legs are getting a stronger dose of those burning rays than your face, so don't push it to the outer limits.

That doesn't mean, of course, that you have to abandon the luxury of a deck chair in less than half an hour. The commercial sunblocks now on the market can be spread on your skin when you've reached your tanning quotient for the day, and you can safely continue to loll. Or you can slip into a light cotton coverup that lets your skin feel the caressing warmth of the tropic sun without its burning rays. Or you can simply turn your deck chair around, so you are lying in shade rather than sun.

Be sybaritic, but don't be silly.

If, however, you ignore our advice, or fall asleep in the inviting sunshine, here is the very best treatment for a really bad case of sunburn. It comes from Dr. J. Melvin Young of Pensacola, Florida, and can be mixed from ingredients you have in your own toilet kit or can easily get from the ship's dispensary or convenience store. Take a dozen aspirin and let them soften for a few minutes in a pint of milk of magnesia or some other liquid antacid. Pat the gritty solution onto the sunburned skin by hand, and leave it on overnight or until the hurts stops. Then wash it off. It's a bit messy, but one application is almost always enough to stop all the pain.

17 Paying the Piper: Tips on Tips

Although the ticket price you pay for your cruise is an all-inclusive charge, there are extras: what you spend at the casino, at the bar, at the shops. Another add-on is tips for the whole army of attendants who have been making the vacation at sea such a carefree time. If you budget your total tipping at 5 percent of your ticket cost, it will be enough to cover all the "necessaries" and to be generous to the stewards who have been particularly helpful to you.

The only circumstance in which that 5 percent won't quite stretch: a passenger traveling alone in a minimum-rate cabin. Fair or unfair, a couple pooling its tips can get by with a little less per person than a passenger on his or her own.

The rule of thumb for many years has been that the standard tip for your cabin steward is $1.50 per person for each day of the cruise. The same amount would go to your dining room steward. But with inflation eating away at the value of that dollar and a half, it's on the low side today. Stewards—with some justice—expect somewhat more, at least from passengers traveling in more expensive cabins. The 5 percent amount should let most passengers pay closer to $2.50 a day, say $30 per couple for a seven-day cruise.

The waiter should take care of the busboy out of your tip. But sometimes the busboy, rather than merely clearing away dirty dishes, has acted like an assistant waiter, bringing your coffee, keeping the bread tray filled, perhaps joking with the children. In that case, you should give him an individual *pourboire*.

Some ships still provide cabin boys to back up the room stewards. If you are lucky enough to have this extra luxury, tip the cabin boy about half what you give to the room steward, but, of course, the tip to the room steward can then be at the low end of the range. Sometimes the more expensive cabins are served by both a steward and stewardess; they would both get roughly equal tips, but somewhat less than you would give to a steward that had to handle the job all by himself.

A person traveling alone should probably tip about 50 percent more than the per person rate advised for a couple.

The tips to your cabin steward and waiter are more or less mandatory. The only exception would be if you are really displeased with their service, in which case you should have arranged for a change early in the trip anyway. But there are a lot of other persons who might come in for a small slice of the 5 percent pool you have set aside, depending on just how much service they have given you.

• The *maître d'* need not be tipped if he has merely greeted you each evening and asked polite questions about how much you enjoyed your dinner. But if he has found a new table for you or fixed you up with par-

ticularly companionable mealtime company, or arranged for a special dish to be prepared just for your party, a tip of $5 or $10 is appropriate. Make it more if you have presented him with special problems or if you want him to remember you fondly when you sail that line again.

• Your *deck steward* may have been taken care of generously enough if you have ordered frequent afternoon drinks from him, and tipped him each time you paid for your piña colada or rum punch. But if you haven't been imbibing, give him a few dollars at journey's end. North Cape cruises and those to Alaska, where the cool sea breezes make you happy to have an attentive deck steward wrap you in woolly blankets, call for a bit more generosity than warmer routes, where the deck stewards supply fewer personal attentions.

• The *pool attendant* or *gymnasium supervisor* need not be tipped for doing their minimal duties: handing you a towel when you clamber out of the pool, or showing you where the weights are kept. But if you have made special demands of them, you should be ready to include a small tip in your farewell.

• *Waiters* and *bartenders* in the various ship lounges will be tipped when you pay for each drink, if the line does not let you merely sign for the drinks. If you do run up a tab and settle it on the final day, you can distribute the tips then. But that is practical only if you carve out a favorite watering spot and give a lot of business to the same attendants. Tips here run a bit less than on land; a 10 percent add-on is not considered stingy.

- The *sommelier,* or wine steward, will present a bill for all your dining room wine and drink orders, and you will simply increase that bill by somewhere between 10 and 15 percent as a tip. If you spend a great deal of time with him discussing the wine stock, or otherwise put him to unusual trouble, it would be a good idea to hand him a $5 or $10 bill right then, which would be in addition to the tip at the end of the cruise. However, it is the rare passenger who demands that much personalized service.

- *Hairdressers, masseuses,* and other such service persons would be tipped just as you would on land.

If you have any doubts about the appropriate tip, there is always someone at the purser's office to give you specific advice.

Except for the tips you give at the time a service is performed, such as those to bartenders, barbers, and sauna attendants, the time for tipping is the final night before you get into home port. With spreading informality, no one will turn their back on raw cash, but it is nicer to follow the custom and present the tips in plain white envelopes: Bring a small supply with you, or gather them up early in the trip from the ship writing room. On the day of the night tips are due, everyone makes a beeline for the writing desks, and the envelope supply is invariably exhausted.

If the cruise is going to last for more than two weeks, hand out tips around halfway through covering services until then, and then again on the final night. But you might put a bit more than half of what you intend to give in the first envelope. If you sign on for one of those long jaunts around the world or through the Straits of Magellan, it's nice to tip every two weeks or so: Crew members spend in the ports of call, too.

Those are the general rules, but there are exceptions. That's why it's good to check with your ship's purser. For instance, Scandinavian ships add a service charge to the drink bills, so no further tips for lounge waiters are required. The Greek stewards' union requires that all tips are pooled, so you simply give a total amount to the chief steward.

Some lines try to snuff out tipping entirely. Holland America has led in this trend, but, truth to tell, stewards on its ships still expect a little cash parting gift. But half of what you would otherwise tip is certainly ample. Tipping is also discouraged on Russian ships as being contrary to principles of social equality. Attendants there won't have their hands out, but they will take tips when they are offered; they usually, though, then turn around and buy a souvenir at the shipboard gift shop as a present for the tipping passengers.

One aspect of tipping on which there is no line-to-line variation, however, is the list of no-no's. It would be gauche to offer a tip to any ship officer. And the cruise director and his staff are there to give their absolute all for you, with no tips expected.

Ports of Call:
Beaches,
Bargains,
Bewitchments

18 Sightseeing in Style

In today's world of jet travel, an important aspect of geography, the space between places, becomes wildly distorted. We tend to measure space in time, and with airplanes flying faster to farther spots, it's hard to get a sense of just how distant a faraway locale is. A special value of sea travel is that it puts a real meaning of distance back onto the map.

"There is a story about a man who remarked to a friend that he had just returned from a vacation on the Cayman Islands and who, when asked where those islands are, replied: 'I don't know; I flew.' " Mabel C. Simmons, travel editor of the New Orleans *Times-Picayune,* tells that tale to highlight the difference between that kind of trip and the one she took aboard the Russian liner *Odessa.* "I can tell you the location," she says. She and her fellow passengers "have been there and we know that the Cayman Islands are in the Caribbean Sea between Jamaica and Mexico."

That sense of geographical exactitude is one reason vacationers choose a cruise, and, having gotten to their scheduled ports through a significant amount of sailing, they want to see what pleasures are there to behold. The ship provides a self-contained world of fun, but it is a journey as well, and most travelers want to explore the place they've come to.

The easiest way to make that exploration is in the packaged tours that will be for sale aboard ship, run either by the cruise line itself or by a tourist operation exclusively picked by the line. You almost always have to sign up for these tours in advance, and at many ports a variety of itineraries and lengths will be offered.

Whether or not you should choose a packaged shore tour depends on a number of factors, starting with your own personality. Do you hate to make decisions or does your everyday life force so much decision making

149

on you that the choicest thing about vacationing is the freedom from choosing? Do you feel hesitant and unsure in strange or exotic surroundings or in trying to communicate in a language other than English? Are you a serious sightseer, who considers a vacation a failure if you miss a prime attraction?

If your answers are yeses, it sounds as though you should take the ship's tours. For a few dollars, all details will be taken care of, you'll hit the top spots on each island, your questions will get answered, and you'll get back to the ship on time and in good condition. Our friend Judith H. Dobrzynski, author of the book *Fasting*, adds another plus of taking a tour: They are usually run in small groups, with a different makeup at each port, so they provide an ideal way to meet more of your fellow passengers.

If, on the other hand, regimentation is your idea of hell, if you like to stop and rest when you want to rest, and hurry through spots that don't catch your fancy, if you like to chat with local residents and seek out unusual byways, then you should probably strike out on your own when your ship pulls into the harbor. If you have special interests, such as visiting churches or haunting antique shops for old jewelry, you also will probably be happier shunning the tours. Lazyheads, too, often decide not to take tours, since those leaving in the morning have a way of leaving very early indeed: 8:00 A.M. departures are common, and some start as early as 7:00, after a special 6:30 breakfast.

But there are ports where even the most resolute opponent of group activity should at least give serious thought to taking a tour. On many of the Greek islands, as we have noted, ships stop for only a few hours, and there is a wealth of antiquities to see. Chances are good that you have picked the cruise in the first place because you are eager to see the evidence of the culture of twenty-five centuries ago, and the surest way to do that is to take the tour. Because many of the sites are miles from the port itself, getting there yourself is impractical. In Rhodes, for instance, on a five-hour stop the typical Chandris tour crisscrosses the island, including both the ancient ramparts of the city of Rhodes and the ruins of Lindos, the most important of the three Dorian cities on the island: an itinerary we would hate to have you miss or try to cover on your own.

When you have chosen a cruise with professors or other learned lecturers aboard, of course you will miss some of the benefits if you opt not to go along on the shore excursions they conduct. But Dobrzynski advises that there are times when it is better to join the group being shepherded by local guides rather than the one with the shipboard expert: The crew member has a broader general knowledge, but often doesn't know as much about a specific port as the guide who lives there and gives tours of nothing else.

Since the length of the group tours, the complexity of the arrangements, and the amount of travel involved vary widely, it is no surprise that the prices do too. A half day of sightseeing in the port city itself should cost less than $10, and on some lines the cost can be as little as $5. You can pick the mode of touring that you like best, with little thought to its pocketbook impact. But there are day-long tours that can come to $100 per couple—from Odessa to Leningrad, say, or visiting the oasis of Marrakesh while the ship is anchored at Casablanca—and require your weighing seriously whether the experience is worth that much money to you. Often a feel of the foreign land you are visiting can be absorbed a lot nearer to the port, and the money you save can be translated into gifts to take home to keep the memories shining.

At some stops, though, the port is little more than a gateway to a major attraction. We have felt sorry for British travelers who chose to see what they could of Florida on foot when their ship pulled into Port Everglades: acre upon acre of storage tanks and warehouses, with none of the atmosphere of sun and fun that draws millions to Florida every year. Elsewhere, La Guaira, for instance, the usual stopping point in Venezuela, is just a bustling port town. Most visitors want to see the capital of Caracas, with Simón Bolívar's home, glass factories, and plush residential sections; the least burdensome way to get there is to sign on for the tour that starts with a ride through the mountains on an air-conditioned bus. Similarly, the car-and-air-taxi tour of the Mayan pyramids at Chichén Itzá is a major reason for a cruise ship's calling at Cozumel, but would hardly be recommended as an independent venture.

Mary McFadden says that the flights over the ice fields around Juneau were one of the highlights of her cruise into the North Pacific aboard the *Royal Viking Sea*. But the small bush aircraft have very limited passenger capacity, so it's a sight you not only have to take as a package, but as a package that fills up quickly and must be signed up for early in the voyage.

There are local boat trips, too, that provide you with a point of view you could never get on your own. When its ships stop in Istanbul, for instance, Lauro Line offers a four-hour orientation tour that concludes with a trip on the Bosporus from Cengelkoy back to your ship that provides a memorable sighting of the fortress of Rumeli Hisar. In Bermuda, Holland America sells scenic cruises on boats especially built to ply shallow waters, that give vacationers glimpses of the private showplace homes at Ridell's Bay and Bootleggers Cave that are inaccessible to public viewing from the land side. In Martinique, Sitmar runs a tour on a raft, complete with a bar, shaded lounging areas, and a steel-drum band, that sails from Fort-de-France to a secluded beach; as on the bush airplanes in Alaska, space is limited on the raft, so you should sign on early.

It is common at ports with clear waters and fascinating underwater formations—particularly in the U.S. Virgin Islands—to have "tours" that are primarily instruction in snorkeling or scuba diving. By all means try these if you swim well and are intrigued by the sport but have never had the opportunity to learn. The instruction is highly professional and far easier to arrange ahead of time on shipboard than after the ship docks.

Tours can provide a margin of safety, ensuring that you'll get to see what you really want to. For, as Rosalind Massow points out, "smaller ports with special attractions can't cope with hundreds of people who want to do the same things at the same time. They don't have enough seats on local planes, enough comfortable cars, and yes, maybe even enough camels," and the priority goes to those who have signed on for the packaged expeditions.

There are other kinds of safety, too, that can be provided by tours. The social safety for an older woman without an escort who wants to enjoy the fun of a local calypso nightclub in Nassau or the gambling halls and extravagant nightclub show at the casino there. Or the actual physical safety of travelers hesitant to venture on their own into native quarters in North African cities. Chances are good that there are no real dangers lurking in the shadows, but you are on vacation, and if worrying is going to dull your fun, go along with a guide and a group.

As we've suggested, the tours are not all devoted to vigorous sightseeing; some are designed for nothing more than fun, a continuation of the partying of shipboard to a new setting. Often the "tour" is merely a trip to a nearby resort hotel, where the cruise line has arranged for some chang-

ing facilities, a private portion of the beach, and perhaps a bar and lunch. One of the nicest such jaunts is designed by Sitmar for the stop at Puerto Vallarta, Mexico; it includes a trip on a large yacht along portions of the Mexican coast you would never otherwise get to see, a three-hour stop for sunning and swimming at picturesque Yelapa Beach, and then a return cruise to your ship.

Often the group trips will include shows of native entertainments, put together especially for the visiting cruise passengers. If you want to see the ritual stone dance in which Indonesian islanders leap over seven-foot-high barriers, you had best go along on a tour from the *Prinsendam*. A lunchtime floor show of Haitian dancing and singing is put on at Beck's Hotel in Cap Haitien just for visitors from ships docked at the port.

The cruise staff will give you full briefings on each port of call and on what the package tours include. Study the itineraries carefully, especially if you have not done a lot of homework on what the main attractions are at that stop. The details of the group tour will tell you a lot about the pace; some suggest you will be on the run all day, some include time for a leisurely lunch at a top hotel, shopping, even a swim. When you have a choice, opt for the regimen most in tune with your own psyche.

But the details of the tour will also at times hint that you might just as well skip the formalities and strike out on your own. When you see, for instance, that most of the tour of Dubrovnik is on foot among the sights of the old town—Sponza Palace, Onofrio fountain, the Dominican and Francisan monasteries—that lie near the waterfront area, you might decide that you can do it all just as easily on your own, at your own pace. Holland America frankly advises vacationers on its cruises to Bermuda that the capital of Hamilton "is best toured on foot." The ships dock right at Front Street in the middle of downtown, and the exhibitions of the historical society, the cathedral, and the parliament buildings are all within easy walking distance. So, of course, are the shops featuring the best English woolens and bone china.

Or in a port like San Juan, Puerto Rico, where taxis are abundant, a city tour of the old section, the modern university, and the prettiest residential sections might be more your style in a cab with a driver who lets you linger where your curiosity is keenest, and can skip entirely points of interest (perhaps the Eleanor Roosevelt slum-clearance project) which just do not interest you.

Taxis are not the only way to get around, of course. You can arrange car rentals, reserving in advance through the major U.S. car-rental outfits if you know ahead of time that you want to drive yourself around. In such tourism-conscious places as Bermuda, there are marinas that will rent you little Sun Fish boats to sail for yourself, or provide licensed fishing guides with their own boats who can take you out to search for tuna or marlin. The *Azur* offers an alternative we believe is unique in the world of cruises: It carries a fleet of bicycles on board so passengers can poke around the byways of the ports of call.

At many of the resort islands, the hotels have arrangements for day visitors to pay a modest fee for use of the locker room and swimming facilities; the cruise director will be able to give you details if you ask. Vir-

tually any hotel will sell you a meal. And at islands such as St. Martin, the public beaches right next to the pier where your tender docks are just lovely and little used except by fellow cruise passengers (and those from other liners that may be calling at the island the same day you are).

Doing a port on your own does not have to mean doing it all by yourself. During the cruise, you will meet others with similar tastes, and you all may want to team up on a shore expedition of your own. That gives you the best of both worlds: a more independent itinerary than you can get in a group, but others to share the fun—and expense—of getting around in an exotic land and seeing vivid flowers and breathtaking panoramas. If you try a group tour and find it grates, look around for others that seem to be fidgeting at the guide's detailed explanation of some eighteenth-century battle, then suggest to the fidgeters that you team up at the next stop in hiring your own wheels and seeing the sights you want to see.

We repeat that the right mode of touring in port depends on your own personality, but generally we would recommend taking a tour in places where the culture is very alien and/or there are a lot of really first-rate sights to see, and striking out on your own at most Caribbean stops and other places where the natives are used to dealing with Americans and you are more interested in the atmosphere than seeing particular buildings or ruins.

But when you are on your own, you do have to watch some things that the tour leaders will take care of for those traveling in groups. Foremost of these is getting back to the ship on time. Don't laugh; the ship's personnel do not check you off or on, you are told specifically when embarkation is, and if you are left behind you'll have to pay your own way to the next port where you can pick up the ship. The problem of getting back on board on time is most intense when the time on the island is an hour or even more behind the time being observed on board your ship. It happens. The clock in the store says 4:30, and you figure that you have an hour to get back to your liner, just as you hear the blast of its whistle and see it begin to pull away from the dock. Remember to set your watch against a shipboard clock before going ashore, and be sure not to change it while you are in port.

Rosalind Massow suggests another caution that passengers venturing into port on their own should heed: Be supercareful about eating salads and other raw vegetables or drinking the water (or anything cooled with chunks of ice made from the water). There are obviously totally safe ports: Vancouver, say, or Bermuda; and you are probably in good hands in large U.S.- or British-run tourist hotels that are likely to have their own water-filtration setups. But otherwise, bend over backward. The lush tropical fruits sold quayside in the Caribbean are tempting, but follow Massow's advice: "Peel your own. Take along a pocketknife and foil-wrapped towelettes, just in case you see some fruit in a market that you must have."

When the liner steams into port, there's another alternative to going with the group or striking out on your own: just stay on board. Don't talk yourself into the state of mind that you've come all this way to reach the destination, so you must explore. You've come all this way to come all this way, with all of the fun in transit. And if going ashore just seems like too much effort, or the charms of the exotic port seems less then entrancing, feel free to stay on board.

The truth is that a lot of the stops, especially in the Caribbean, offer nothing very unique or memorable. John Pinkerman of Copley News Service, for instance, picks Curaçao as an island offering passengers little more than "an opportunity to stretch your legs." And when you see that the chief—in some respects the only—attraction on the packaged tour of Grand Cayman is a visit to a turtle farm, giving you an opportunity, as the brochure puts it, to "learn all the fascinating aspects of green turtles' life cycle," you may decide to stay with the cycle of living you have come to know on your ship. Some cruise itineraries pack in so much—fourteen stops in fourteen days—that you begin to get an if-this-is-Tuesday-it-must-be-Belgium dizziness that a day or two of spurning sightseeing can do wonders to counteract.

Your liner will dock at the wharf in some ports but have to anchor at sea other places, where the harbor is not deep enough for large ships. You will come and go from ship to shore in tenders run frequently all during the stay; the ride can be a bouncy one if the sea is choppy, and might just be enough to make you opt, in a port where it is a close call, for staying on board.

But staying on board is hardly a negative thing. In fact, shipboard life on days in port is to real cruise lovers the epitome of what they want from a vacation. All the services are still available; the sumptuous meals are not one whit less spectacular, and the new movies still show up at their regular times. The one thing missing is a goodly percentage of your fellow passengers. Suddenly the ship seems all yours, like home after a crowd of visitors departs and it's just the family again. Wonderful. To be reveled in. Enjoy!

If you happen to have friends in any of the ports that you are visiting, by all means invite them aboard. You can easily arrange for them to join you for a meal (it will be charged to your account) and they can use the facilities as your guest. You might even hook them on the pleasures of taking a cruise.

19 Shopping with Sense

Second to eating, shopping is probably the cruise activity engaged in by the largest percentage of vacationers. For some it is a major goal: Caribbean liners sailing in the late fall always carry many passengers who are planning to scoop up their entire listful of Christmas presents in the duty-free shops of Charlotte Amalie. For others shopping is a chore and they try to do as little of it as possible. But virtually everyone brings back a few mementos of the cruise and the foreign shores your ship has touched.

There are sure to be a few family members or close friends for whom you will want to bring back an I-was-thinking-of-you gift. And things you buy for yourself, in addition to the basic beauty or ease they can bring, will forever afterward have the special glow of recalling a vacation that we certainly hope has been a high point for you. Things can serve this function even if they have none of the obvious connections with the islands you visit that Jamaican straw handbags or Egyptian galabias do. We bought our Danish dinner china (at a favorable price) in Bermuda, and when we use it we remember with pleasure the blue waters, coral beaches, and gentle air of that enchanting island.

You will get as much advice as you want from the cruise staff on just what to buy at each port of call and where to buy it. Princess Cruises, for instance, gives all passengers a brochure listing the products that local craftsmen are particularly adept at—Eskimo whalebone baskets in Alaska, flamboyant paper flowers in Mexico—and where the taxing policy provides big bargains on such imported wares as Dutch dolls in Aruba or Swiss watches in Panama.

As the value of the U.S. dollar has fallen against other major currencies, some of the bargains available in foreign lands have disappeared. But there are still items that not only capture the special talents of the countries you are visiting but that cost a fraction of what they would in U.S. stores. And one of the joys of vacationing by ship is that you can bring along with you merchandise like the prized Mapuche Indian rugs from Chile that would be, at best, an awful nuisance for an air traveler.

Other purchases that *Business Week* magazine says are still good buys around the world include semiprecious stones and bikinis from Brazil; serapes, leather sandals, and onyx chess sets from Mexico; locally made modern jewelry from Greece; copper and brass pieces from Israel; fur hats from Russia, as well as (surprisingly) enameled cast-iron cookware. In the Orient, the magazine recommends finding teak and rosewood furniture from factory outlets in Taiwan, pewter and hand-tailored clothes in Singapore; pearls in Japan; and jade in Hong Kong. The days of finding good prices on made-to-order suits in Hong Kong are over, the editors advise.

Probably the single most popular shopping stop for cruises is St. Thomas in the U.S. Virgin Islands. The local economy has long been based on selling luxury goods from around the world to vacationing Americans, and the ploy is so successful that the island even has a special exemption in U.S. tariff laws, so you can bring more home duty-free from this spot than any other on your travels.

Truth to tell, the bargains in St. Thomas are not all they once were. The change has not come from the island merchants, but from the growth back at home of outlets selling at discount prices. The big advantage that St. Thomas stores have is that they are outside the U.S. customs line, so goods from elsewhere arrive there without any payment of import taxes. To these lower-priced goods, the retailers add a normal markup. On some items long the mainstay of Charlotte Amalie trade, such as cameras and binoculars, that means the final price comes out just about the same as that posted by a discount operation in New York or some other big city, which pays more for the merchandise at wholesale, but sells at lower markup. So how good the prices will look depends a lot on what kind of bargains you can get in your hometown. On the island, a lot of the emphasis has shifted from cameras to luxury European goods not usually sold at low markups in the United States: French couturier showrooms, for example, are booming on St. Thomas, and might be worth checking out.

The one absolutely unquestionable bargain on St. Thomas still is liquor. The prices are startlingly low for virtually all the name brands of whiskey and brandy which the world offers. But that special customs treatment that the Virgins get adds an even bigger inducement: U.S. law ordinarily allows importation of only one quart of liquor duty-free; above that, you have to pay import taxes even if you have bought little else abroad. But there's an exception for booze in the U.S. Virgin Islands; you can bring in a gallon of that, and the stores there even have handy boxes built to hold just five fifths.

Besides the cost saving, there is also available in Charlotte Amalie a

wider variety of enticing liqueurs than you are likely to find at any liquor store in your hometown. And the big St. Thomas outlets provide free sipping. That's how we find a scrumptious caramel vanilla liqueur from Spain that has become a permanent fixture in our liquor closet ever since.

But if you know what you want from the Charlotte Amalie liquor merchants without a stop for sipping, you can handle that part of your shopping without ever setting foot in the store. And that can be a real plus on some winter days when a half-dozen cruise ships all disgorge their passengers at St. Thomas at the same time and everyone heads to buy the bargain booze. We have quite successfully simply written a letter to a liquor store, enclosing an order and a check (carefully dated after we are out of the United States) for what our order would come to based on the most recent prices we had, plus a bit for increases. The order has been delivered to our ship, along with little odds and ends—small bottles of perfume or cologne, mostly—to cover the couple of dollars of overpayment. The extras turned out to be great remembrances for a couple of neighbors or co-workers for whom we had forgotten to get little presents. (Now, we always buy a half dozen of some small, inexpensive item—scarves, or local wood carvings—to have on hand for those we remember too late we should have remembered.)

On a lot of the bigger ships nowadays, it is even easier to avoid standing in line at St. Thomas liquor stores: A representative of one of the big outlets gets aboard in San Juan, distributes price lists, takes orders and checks, and disembarks at Charlotte Amalie; the store then delivers the liquor to the ship, and the stewards bring it to your cabin.

That sort of arrangement raises a question that is the subject of hot controversy in the travel business: whether someone among the cruise staff, or the line itself, is getting a rake-off from the purchases you make at the store they recommend. Certainly on some lines everyone is as clean as hounds' teeth and have no financial connection to the outlets to which they steer passengers, but don't count on it.

On the other hand, don't automatically consider it a rip-off and go out of your way to shop at an outlet where the price you pay will not include a "commission" for the person who recommended it. (In fact, if you take a group tour, it may be difficult to have time for shopping except at the store at which the guide has planned for you all to browse.) It probably does mean that you are paying more than you might have to for similar items at other shops, but in at least two respects there's a good side to dealing with the retailers recommended by the ship's company: You can count on their being reputable merchants selling you items which are in fact what they are passed off to be; that's a major consideration if you are buying semiprecious stones or antiques, the kind of product where it's easy to fool a novice with a good fake. The other plus: You can take complaints not to a store owner, who knows he is unlikely ever to see you again, but to a cruise staff that carries real clout, because literally thousands of future customers can be shut off.

If you know a lot about the merchandise you are looking for—if you devote time to studying primitive wood carving, say—then you should shy away from the spots guides will be promoting and seek out other merchants. And if your port is a major city, you can head for the major stores and shop with confidence. But in a smaller spot, where the chances of your getting taken with unfamiliar merchandise are greater, patronizing the establishment shops may end up costing you a few bucks more, but it can also save you from being rooked out of a lot more than a few bucks.

The price you pay for goods in foreign ports may be only part of your total costs. There are U.S. import duties to consider. The regulations on what travelers can bring into the country without paying extra tariffs became significantly more liberal in 1978, so for those doing only a modest amount of shopping on a cruise, they no longer have to be a worry. But if you are planning to make major purchases, knowing the rules in advance may save you a lot of money.

Start with the basic rule that you can bring back to the States, duty-free, $300 worth of goods bought abroad, valued at their fair retail value. In almost all cases, that will be the price you paid for them, unless your Uncle Harry owns a store in Acapulco and sold you things at below cost. In practice, the exemption for a family traveling together is all lumped together, so a couple has a $600 allowance, which goes up to $900 if they have a child with tham, even if the child is only an infant. (Until the change, the limit for skipping the import tax was only $100.)

There's one exception to the $300 rule: It is doubled for goods bought in the U.S. Virgin Islands (or in American Samoa or Guam, which are seldom cruise stops). That means that you can each bring back $600 worth of merchandise bought in St. Thomas duty-free, or $300 worth of merchandise bought there and $300 worth bought in other ports. (But buy $400 worth in other places and $200 in the Virgins, and $100 of that will be dutiable.)

As we have said, the amount of liquor you can include in your duty-free exclusion is limited. So, now is the number of cigarettes—a limitation that may catch you unaware, since it was only recently imposed. You can claim only 200 cigarettes a person (that's one carton) under your exemption.

As before, you have to be out of the States for forty-eight hours to get the duty-free exemption, and cannot have used it anytime in the preceding thirty days. If you make a business trip to Montreal shortly before leaving on your cruise, be sure not to claim your exemption to bring in a $20 gift you bought, or you will lose the entire $300/$600 exemption on your cruise.

The new law not only upped the value of duty-free merchandise that can be brought in, but it changed the way tariffs are imposed on the rest. Before, the merchandise brought in by vacationers was treated just like goods bought by an importer for resale, according to complicated formulas that first have to classify each item, then apply different percentages or flat dollar duties on them. Now, once your duty-free allocation is used up, the next $600 worth of dutiable merchandise *per person* will be assessed at the flat rate of 10 percent. But that boon is only for merchandise that vacationers bring back with them: another plus of ocean-going. (The St. Thomas lobby got special treatment on this point, too: Goods bought in the Virgin Islands that are over the exemption limit are taxed at only 5 percent, and can be mailed back rather than having to accompany the traveler.)

Items that you are having shipped home, or that are over the $600 flat-rate limit for dutiable merchandise, will be taxed at the regular rate that applies to commercial imports. On some items that you can buy considerably cheaper abroad, that won't be a major deterrent: Leather handbags, for instance, carry a tariff of between 8.5 percent and 10 percent, chocolate bars of 5 percent, wood carvings of 8 percent. But on others the import is significant: Wool sweaters, for example, are weighed, and the duty is 37.5 cents per pound, plus 20 percent of your purchase price. Hand-embroidered cotton handkerchiefs cost 40 percent of their value plus another 4 cents each. Inexpensive sets of china plates can be slapped with a tariff of 48 percent of the retail price, plus 10 cents per dozen pieces.

The tariff on liquor isn't a pocketbook crunch—most often just a dime a fifth—but the Internal Revenue tax that all hard stuff over your quota has to pay can really ad up: It's more than $2 a bottle.

Those rates only come into play if you go over your allowances. But many cruise passengers plan in advance to use the vacation as an opportunity to pick up in Curaçao that fine Swiss watch they have long wanted, or to splurge with gift money on a diamond cocktail ring from Israel. Even a 10 percent duty is too high if you can avoid it. And you may be able to.

For one thing, if you see that you are going to go over the exemption limit, you can arrange to have presents you bought for others mailed back to the States. The bigger stores that cater to cruise passengers will be equipped to do this. If the value of the gift is less than $25, it comes in duty-free and doesn't count toward your total. The limit is $40 for mailings from the U.S. Virgins. While it is unlikely that the Customs Bureau is going to probe too deeply into your motivations on gifts of this size, you should know that the provision is only for "bona fide gift parcels"—if a friend asked you to pick up something and gave you the money to buy it, don't flaunt that fact.

The other way to save on duties is to buy merchandise on which there is no tariff. Generally, antiques (anything over 100 years old) and works of art fall within this category. So do postage stamps and books by foreign authors or in a language other than English, as well as a host of other items if bought from poorer countries than the United States is trying to help by something called the Generalized System of Preferences, but few travelers know about this loophole. The ignorance is not the fault of the Customs Bureau, which will send its flyer on GSP to anyone who writes (to Washington, D.C. 20229) and asks for it.

GSP provides that there will be no import taxes on certain kinds of goods from certain countries. Many cruise stops are among those countries, including Hong Kong and Singapore; Senegal; Morocco, Egypt, Israel, and Turkey; Yugoslavia; Mexico, Brazil, the Bahamas, and virtually all of the Caribbean islands. Even Bermuda is listed as one of the "beneficiary countries." There's quite a long list of merchandise that qualifies for the duty-free treatment from these ports, including most precious jewelry, china figurines and other ornamental pieces, perfume, furs, pearls, wooden furniture, printed matter, and bamboo and rattan items other than furniture.

No textiles fall under the scheme, even if the cloth has been made into clothing. But the biggest catch to the arrangement is that the merchandise has to have been "grown, manufactured, or produced" in the country where you buy it. That means you cannot stock up on French perfume in one of the Netherlands Antilles and hope to bring it in under GSP. Generally on smaller purchases, unless the products have obviously been imported by the GSP country, the customs officials will take your word that they are native-made. But on purchases of more than $250, ask the seller to give you a Certificate of Origin (called "Form A"). If he doesn't know what you are talking about, reconsider whether you want to make a purchase of more than $250 there. One of the extra advantages of buying GSP goods is that they come in duty-free even if you have them shipped, but in those cases, they must have a Form A and a commercial invoice, regardless of the value of the purchase.

There's one more aspect of customs rules you have to know about while doing your shopping: There are some foreign purchases that you cannot bring into the United States at all. Two that most often trouble Caribbean cruise passengers are tortoiseshell items and goatskin (which is often used as the hide of souvenir voodoo drums in Haiti, for instance), but there are a variety of others. Bringing plants into the United States is so complicated that you may as well consider them a prohibited product and not try to bring home the exotic greenery you see in the tropics. The same goes for fish and wildlife: A cruise is not a good place to add to your tropical fish collection or procure a cage-mate for your parakeet. Fireworks, switchblade knives, absinthe, and obscene publications are other items that are banned. More likely to be bothersome is the requirement that much pre-Columbian art can come in only if the Latin American country in which it originates provides you with an export authorization. If you are shopping for such items, buy only from established dealers, and ask about whether a certificate is required.

One other troublesome import bar has been made somewhat less troublesome in the new customs law. This is the right given to trademark owners to set limits on tourist imports of products bearing their brand name. That means, the manufacturers say, that you cannot bring in any Crepe de Chine or 1000 de Jean Patou perfume, for instance, or Mario

Buccellati or Etienne Aigner jewelry, or Arriflex cameras or lenses. But Congress has now decided that, regardless of what the manufacturers say, you can bring in *one* package of any "no consent" item, as long as it is for your personal use (which includes gift giving, but not selling it to someone else). What if you try to bring in two bottles of 1000 de Jean Patou? Chances are that you'll get away with it, but we would advise against trying; the customs inspector might insist on the second bottle being destroyed right at the pier, and where would your fabulous free-port saving be then?

Customs aren't the only censors of what you can take home, of course. You may see a spouse's face fall when you unveil the find of your independent shopping tour ashore. Or, what happens even more, three days after the scent of the tropical flowers has faded, you come to hate the very piece of native carving you cherished so on the island, and you can't figure out why you bought it in the first place. Don't despair. At least some cruises end up with white elephant sales.

The way they are run on the *Sun Viking*, the traveler who has some object he or she wants to get rid of—there's no requirement that it have been purchased en route—registers it at the cruise office, with a minimum acceptable price. Then an auction is held, where each white elephant goes to the highest bidder; if no one is willing to pay the minimum price, the piece goes back to its owner. It is run as a fun activity, with no auctioneer's commission. And a white elephant sale, besides letting you unload your mistakes, can let you pick up a choice item or two that is simply not appreciated by the original purchaser. That way, if you opted to stay aboard and loll in the sun while the liner was docked at some minor island, you can still bring home a native knicknack and no one will ever know that the island sands never touched your sandals.

20 Hassle-Free Homecoming

The end of a cruise is always a bit bittersweet. If all has gone as it should, you have been living in a fantasy world, disconnected from the cares and concerns of your "real" world. Suddenly it is time to rejoin that other world, the domain of rules and regulations, and as if to make sure you know it, your last hours aboard ship are plunged into a pile of forms and procedures. It's not really so bad, but it is an abrupt change.

Certainly the cruise staff does everything possible to make reentry as painless as possible. Both your daily ship newspaper and a lecture by the cruise director will clue you on the proper way to get through all the regulatory red tape, and if those presentations don't answer all your questions, the cruise director and his assistants are available to handle individual inquiries. Some of your fellow passengers will have tips on how to deal with customs, too, but be cautious about listening to any of them, especially if they involve cutting corners. Yes, they might have gotten away with it in the past, but no, the risk isn't worth it to you.

There are two branches of the U.S. government that you have to deal with before you head homeward. The easier is the Immigration Service. On many cruises, for U.S. citizens who are merely returning to the port from which they left a week or two earlier, there's no checking at all. (The inspectors have records from the time you boarded, of course.) On some longer cruises, or for passengers who joined the ship somewhere en route, the inspectors will want to see some form of proof that you are a citizen—a passport, birth certificate, naturalization papers, voting registration card. Even travelers who are not U.S. citizens will have to go through minimal formalities: Simply present your landing card. Almost always, the Immigration clearance is done on board your liner, in one of the public rooms.

The more involved clearance is from the Customs Bureau, but on many lines this, too, is now mostly handled on the ship. The night before you are scheduled to dock, your steward will give you a customs declaration form. Fill it out completely, one form per family. You must list everything you acquired abroad, even if it was a gift rather than something you bought yourself. List the price you paid, and make a fair estimate if the item is a gift. Don't forget to include items of clothing you have started to wear, or perfume that has been added to your cosmetic kit. Again, the likelihood of the customs inspectors ferreting out an individual opened bottle of perfume are remote, but the possible losses in time and money are just not worth the chance.

The new law that liberalized the duty-free minimums for vacationers also stiffened the penalty for "misrepresenting" an item on your declaration: Now, you may have to pay a penalty as well as the duty due. So say just what it is and what it cost. But you can and should describe the item in a way that will highlight its duty-free status, if in fact it fits into such a category. Describe the print as "original lithograph, hand-printed" to emphasize that it is fine art and not a commercial reproduction. Describe the onyx chess set as "game, played on board, made in GSP country (Mexico)" to parrot the language of the tariff schedule itself. And, while it is not required, it would be wise to pull together your receipts for all your purchases and have them handy when the inspectors go over your form.

The next thing to do, after filling in the customs declaration, is pack up. It's rather a nuisance, but an inevitability of ship travel: The luggage is picked up the night before disembarkation, often as early as 5:00 P.M., so the crew can get it arranged and ready to go onto the pier as soon as the ship docks. (Even with the preparation, it generally takes two hours to unload the luggage.) Fill in completely the luggage tags the steward will have given you along with your customs forms, and put one on each piece of luggage. At some ports, these tags will be coded with the first letter of your last name, at others with a primary color. Be sure to remember your color; in fact, it's best to slip an extra tag into your disembarkation papers, so you won't be able to forget.

Of course, you must not pack those papers—your passport and such. You also keep out nightclothes, toiletries, the clothes you plan to wear for landing, and the clothes for your last evening on board (which is always quite informal, given the packing constraints). But anything you do not pack and leave for the steward the night before you will have to carry off yourself in the morning.

In addition to the last-minute necessities, you may want to carry fragile or oddly shaped purchases that don't fit easily into suitcases. Many lines strongly urge you to carry off your own liquor purchases and cigarettes. The problem is that so many passengers have similar-looking packages that the ship managers insist they cannot guarantee that someone will not walk off with your package from the dock, before you get there. Most passengers heed the advice, although we have had the liquor taken off with the baggage and had no troubles. The five-pack boxes are heavy, especially if you have two or more. You'll have to weigh for yourself how much the convenience of having them unloaded for you is worth against the risk of losing your purchase.

On the actual morning of landing, different ships and different ports handle customs clearance in different ways. You are luckiest if you are on a liner using what the Treasury calls the V-PACC procedure. That stands for Vessel Passenger Accelerated Customs Clearance, and it means for approximately three-quarters of the vacationers involved that they can handle all formalities on board, without ever having to open a bag. The customs inspectors will set up shop in one of the public rooms, go over your customs form with you, and then give you time to catch a quick breakfast or pack your final hand-carried bag. If you can manage it, it is best to have both husband and wife together at the inteview; if not, be sure the one there has all the details about all purchases made by both of you.

In about an hour and a half, names of individual passengers will be called, and that means you are free to leave. Go to the luggage area on the dock, identify your bags, get a porter, and be on your way. Only a minority will be asked to let inspectors actually see their bags. It is the most hassle-free way to get through Customs, but it does have its price: You have to be on time for the on-board inspection of your declaration form, and those interviews are often set as early as 6:00 A.M.

For ships not using the V-PACC procedure, the actual customs inspection takes place on the pier: You find your bags, and get them together with an inspector, who will then go over your declaration. He or she may ask you to open all your luggage and let it be thoroughly examined, but that is not likely: It probably means that the service got a tip that someone who fits your general description was going to try to smuggle in some illegal drugs, or it may be that you appear unusually nervous. For most passengers, a quick look inside one randomly selected bag is all that is needed.

Under either system, you will find your luggage among the thousands of suitcases by going to the area marked with either the color of your tag or the first letter of your last name. Since so many pieces look alike, be sure to check that the ones you pick really have your name on them; be especially careful if you have had liquor boxes taken off with the luggage. If you have spent more on merchandise broad than the duty-free allowance, of course, you will have to pay the tariff on it; there will be a cashier's window handy to make your payment, and the inspector will make it as light as possible by counting the items with the stiffest import taxes among those that the duty-free exemption covers. The tariff payments can be made by personal check, as well as cash or traveler's checks, as long as you are not asking for change of more than $50 from the traveler's checks.

If you bring in more than $5,000 in what the lawmakers call "monetary instruments" (currency, traveler's checks, money orders, bearer bonds, or the like), you must fill out Customs Form 4790. There's no bar to bringing the money in, or import tax on it, but it is against the law not to file the form, and it could even lead to criminal prosecution. We have never known anyone to return from vacation with $5,000 in cash, but someone hits it lucky in those casinos in Puerto Rico and the Bahamas, so it just might be you.

It's hard to plan in advance just when you will get in, given the uncertainties of sea currents and the like. One line tells passengers they may get off at Miami as early as 8:00 in the morning or as late as 11:00. If you are having folks meet you, they can get a reading by calling the line the day before, but even that won't be precise. If the ship isn't using the V-PACC system, you have more choice about when to get off, and you can always opt to make it later rather than earlier: That not only means you will have less of a wait to find an inspector who is not busy, but it lets you be more precise about what time friends should show up.

If you have driven to the pier and parked nearby, the porters will either take your luggage right to your car or show you someplace where you can drive up next to it and open your trunk. If you want to have a rental car ready at the dock, tell the cruise director at least by the day before, and he'll arrange it. Given the bustle and inevitable letdown of coming home, the most graceful way to reenter is to have a limousine and driver meet you at the ship; given what the entire trip has cost you, that won't add much extra, and it will be a welcome luxury. If winnings in a casino or thrift in the duty-free shops has left a few more dollars in your pocket than you expected at trip's end, go ahead and hire a car and chauffeur. The cruise staff will gladly arrange that, too.

Then home, and unpacking, and giving out the gifts, and recounting the story of your voyage to those who are good enough friends to hear it for the fifth time. It should have been a very special window in your year.

We hope you found relaxation and romance, adventure and insight, that you supped at the fun and drank at the opportunities for quiet reflection. And that the very next day after you get home, you'll go out and buy a big piggy bank and start saving for your next cruise. It's hard to believe, but it will be even better.

Index